Generative AI in the English Composition Classroom

Designed to cater to the needs of both novice and seasoned writing instructors, this book provides a range of practical and adaptable strategies for integrating generative artificial intelligence (AI) into English writing curricula.

Generative AI in the English Composition Classroom proposes strategic methodologies to ensure that AI is utilized as a facilitator of learning and creativity, rather than as a shortcut to academic success. With a particular emphasis on sophisticated large language models such as Claude, ChatGPT, and Gemini, this book critically addresses potential challenges, including concerns related to academic integrity. It includes case studies and practical strategies to exemplify how AI can enhance the writing process while emphasizing the continuing importance of a solid foundation in writing structure, processes, and rhetorical strategies. These case studies and strategies are designed for immediate application, offering educators and students practical tools to effectively navigate AI-augmented writing environments. Finally, the book looks to the future, discussing the evolving skill sets required in the workforce and how educators can equip students for a future in which AI is an integral component.

A forward-thinking and invaluable guide, this book will be of interest to educators involved in teaching English Composition and writing.

Daniel Plate is Professor of English at Lindenwood University, USA.

Elizabeth Melick is Assistant Professor of English at Lindenwood University, USA.

James Hutson is Professor of Art History and Visual Culture at Lindenwood University, USA.

Susan Edele is Associate Professor of English at Lindenwood University, USA.

Routledge Research in Writing Studies

A Writing Center Practitioner's Inquiry into Collaboration
Pedagogy, Practice, And Research
Georganne Nordstrom

Engaging Research Communities in Writing Studies
Ethics, Public Policy, and Research Design
Johanna L. Phelps

Writing, Imitation, and Performance
Insights from Neuroscience Research
Irene L. Clark

Emotional Value in the Composition Classroom
Self, Agency, and Neuroplasticity
Ryan Crawford

Dialogic Editing in Academic and Professional Writing
Engaging the Trace of the Other
Edited by Özüm Üçok-Sayrak, Janie Harden Fritz and Kristen Lynn Majocha

A Multidisciplinary Exploration into Flow in Writing
Deborah F. Rossen-Knill, Katherine Schaefer, Matthew W. Bayne, Whitney Gegg-Harrison, Dev Crasta, and Alessandra R. Dimauro

Generative AI in the English Composition Classroom
Practical and Adaptable Strategies
Daniel Plate, Elizabeth Melick, James L. Hutson, and Susan Edele

For more information about this series, please visit: www.routledge.com/Routledge-Research-in-Writing-Studies/book-series/RRWS

Generative AI in the English Composition Classroom

Practical and Adaptable Strategies

Daniel Plate, Elizabeth Melick, James Hutson, and Susan Edele

NEW YORK AND LONDON

First published 2025
by Routledge
605 Third Avenue, New York, NY 10158

and by Routledge
4 Park Square, Milton Park, Abingdon, Oxon, OX14 4RN

Routledge is an imprint of the Taylor & Francis Group, an informa business

ISBN: 978-1-032-83135-0 (hbk)
ISBN: 978-1-032-83136-7 (pbk)
ISBN: 978-1-003-50794-9 (ebk)

DOI: 10.4324/9781003507949

Typeset in Times New Roman
by Apex CoVantage, LLC

Contents

About the Authors

Daniel Plate earned his B.A. in English and philosophy from Taylor University in Indiana, an M.F.A. in creative writing from the University of Arkansas, and a Ph.D. in literature from Washington University in St. Louis. He teaches creative writing, literature, and Composition at Lindenwood University. He has published poetry and research in artificial intelligence and pedagogy and splits his time between developing code to support his teaching and doing research in the overlap between AI and innovative pedagogy.

Elizabeth Melick earned her B.A. from Capital University and her M.A. and Ph.D. from Kent State University. The focus of her graduate study was medieval literature, and in 2019, she published an edition of four Middle English romances from the Otuel group with the Middle English Text Series. Dr. Melick is also an active researcher in the area of the scholarship of teaching and learning, where her two primary areas of focus are engaged learning and student support. She serves as Coordinator of first year writing, which combines her interest in pedagogy with her many years of experience in teaching Composition courses.

James Hutson specializes in multidisciplinary research that encompasses artificial intelligence, neurohumanities, neurodiversity, immersive realities, and the gamification of education. Earning a Bachelor of Arts in Art from the University of Tulsa, a Master of Arts in Art History from Southern Methodist University, and a Ph.D. in Art History from the University of Maryland, College Park, he later acquired additional master's degrees in leadership and game design from Lindenwood University and additional Ph.D. in Artificial Intelligence at Capitol Technology University (2023). Over the span of his academic career since 2006, Hutson has held various pedagogical and administrative positions across five universities, including Chair of Art History, Assistant Dean of Graduate and Online Programs, and, most recently, Lead XR Disruptor and Department Head of Art History and Visual Culture. Notably, his scholarly portfolio includes several books on the application of artificial intelligence in education and cultural heritage, as well as numerous articles and case studies.

Susan Edele earned her Bachelor of Science in Education from Truman State University, majoring in mass communications and minoring in English and secondary education. She earned her Master of Arts in English Composition from the University of Missouri – St. Louis, and she earned her Master of Fine Arts in Creative Writing from Lindenwood University. She teaches Composition courses and creative writing courses. She has published flash fiction and nonfiction pieces in literary journals, along with scholarly articles in academic journals. Susan has presented conference sessions on writing and academic support techniques and is an active member in the International Writing Centers Association. Along with teaching, Susan is also the Director of the Lindenwood University Writing Center.

Preface

The words “artificial intelligence” or “AI” appeared over 100 times in the program for the 2024 Conference on College Composition and Communication, and there were more than 20 sessions dedicated to the topic of AI in Composition classrooms. The treatment of AI in these sessions and presentations ranged from strategies for including AI in Composition courses, to suggestions for how instructors can use AI to enhance their teaching materials, to considerations of intellectual property and academic integrity in light of AI. Many of the conversations about AI in these sessions were characterized by curiosity and a cautious hope. However, AI was also a frequent topic of conversation in sessions that were not specifically about AI, where it was invoked as a commonly feared and reviled boogeyman, a looming threat lurking in the corners of our classrooms for which everyone in the field must hold an equal amount of dread.

The stark differences between presenters who have enthusiastically incorporated AI into their Composition courses and those who refuse to allow AI into their classrooms are likely familiar to any Composition instructor who has seen similar conversations play out in departmental meetings and hallway conversations since the launch of OpenAI’s ChatGPT in November 2022. At the time, Stephen Marche’s “The College Essay is Dead,” published in *The Atlantic*, sent waves of panic through higher education communities, with no community feeling the panic so strongly as writing-focused fields like Composition. Many English and Composition instructors rushed to revise writing project assignments ahead of the start of the

Spring 2023 semester so that it might be more difficult for students to rely on AI for passing work; some instructors contemplated relying more heavily on handwritten work to evade the possibility that AI would contribute to students' submissions.

While that early panic eventually subsided and many instructors have begun to embrace (often cautiously) AI in their Composition classrooms, there remains little consensus on how the field of Composition ought to regard AI tools and whether or not they ought to have a place in our Composition courses.

The reality is that, at the time of this book's writing in the Spring of 2024, there remains no reliable or consistent method for detecting writing that was produced or enhanced by an AI tool. Many instructors, particularly writing instructors, believe that they can easily tell when a student used AI to write their work, but research has shown that instructors can really only identify *bad* AI writing; any student who has developed strong skills in using AI will likely escape the notice of their instructor or the detection software. As a result, there is a near certainty that writing produced by AI is present in assignments students submit regardless of whether or not the instructor has welcomed AI in their classroom. In fact, it is most reasonable for instructors to assume that the work their students submit will include text that was generated by an AI tool or may have been planned, outlined, proofread, or edited by an AI tool.

To move beyond worrying about whether or not it's possible to detect AI writing in student work, it's important to acknowledge that how we think about AI in our classrooms must extend beyond the point that we submit final grades at the end of our courses. Many instructors who are still attempting to maintain their Composition classrooms as AI-free spaces are limiting their consideration of the issue to what they believe they can control – what happens in the courses they design and teach. They believe that their students cannot possibly achieve the learning objectives that have traditionally been the purpose of writing courses if AI tools are permitted or welcomed in their classrooms. It is important to consider how we can continue to help our students achieve the learning objectives of

Composition courses as our higher education landscape continues to shift and change, often at an alarming rate. However, this view is unnecessarily narrow. Stubbornly insisting that Composition courses remain unchanged in their learning objectives, methods of instruction, and approaches to assessment will leave students unprepared to meet the challenges and expectations they will encounter in their later coursework (let alone their future careers).

There is much that still must be determined in the discussion of how AI will intersect with education, and indeed, what AI's role will be in our daily lives more broadly. However, there is no evidence to support a vision of the future in which most workers are not permitted to use AI and in which AI has no more than a minimal role in our professional and personal lives. In just the one and a half years since the launch of ChatGPT-3, the infusion of AI has accelerated considerably, with AI tools and LLMs being built into the programs that form the foundation of our everyday workflows, such as our word processors and email systems. These changes are sometimes so subtle as to be barely noticeable – autocomplete functions in text messaging apps have already been incorporating AI into our informal writing processes for years.

While some Composition instructors cling to a concept of writing as a process that is entirely completed by human authors, the world outside of our classroom has already moved on to a system in which writing is driven and guided by humans but completed through a combination of human and AI contributions. Skills in using AI tools are already desirable in various job markets, including the academic job market for Composition faculty – in the Fall of 2023, a competency in generative AI began to be included as a desirable qualification in some job postings in Composition and digital humanities.

This book responds to this precarious and quickly changing moment in Composition instruction by assuming a sense of responsibility to prepare students to write in a world where AI tools are a widely accepted part of the writing process. There are still many thorny issues related to AI and writing, to be sure – these are issues that we, as a field of Writing Studies, will have to grapple with for the decades to come. However, our position is that turning away from AI in our instruction of Composition is not only a futile exercise but also an approach that will disadvantage our students, preventing them from building the knowledge and skills that will help them become nimble writers who can respond effectively to writing tasks in their future careers, many of which will require the use of AI tools.

Our position is that AI ought to be present in college Composition classrooms, both as a topic of discussion and as a tool that is explored, tested, and implemented. Our goal in this book is to help Composition instructors include AI in their Composition instruction through specific strategies and lessons. We also hope that this book invites contemplation on how Composition instruction and the field of Writing Studies can and must evolve in the age of AI.

Whether you have never interacted with an AI tool or you have already begun to incorporate AI in your own work processes and classrooms, we hope this book will offer valuable information, topics for consideration, and easy-to-implement strategies for developing Composition courses that implement AI to the benefit of students.

Acknowledgments

We are grateful to our Lindenwood University community and its many members who have helped us develop our perspectives on teaching with artificial intelligence and supported our work on this project. In particular, we acknowledge Dean Kathi Vosevich of Lindenwood University's College of Arts and Humanities, who has offered support and encouragement for Humanities faculty to explore AI tools and consider how they can be effectively incorporated into our classrooms. The support we have received from our colleagues and college leaders has empowered us to develop the teaching strategies outlined in this book.

We would also like to acknowledge that this project is built on the research and collegial exchange of ideas of colleagues within the wider academic community. Both published research and informal knowledge sharing have helped us to learn about AI and develop our own practice in using AI and teaching with AI.

This book is a testament to the strength of our network and the shared commitment to fostering an environment where students can learn to tell their own stories, armed with the skills to thrive in an age dominated by artificial intelligence.

Introduction

Approaches to AI in Composition

Daniel Plate, Elizabeth Melick, and James Hutson

In the 2023 issue of *Composition Studies*, Gavin Johnson offered a case for "cautious optimism" regarding AI and Writing Studies, which included four tenets for approaching AI and writing rooted in previous scholarship and pedagogy on related topics such as computers and writing and digital rhetorics. These four tenets offer Composition instructors a useful guide for navigating the arrival of AI tools in their writing classrooms. One of Johnson's tenets in particular encapsulates the core rationale for this book: "technologies must be taught." When explaining this tenet, Johnson writes,

> Integration of these technologies into writing curricula signals an investment in extending digital rhetorical skill. To these ends and seeing where we are and divining where we are going in terms of AI and writing, a multiliteracies approach to AI and LLM-generative writing is worthy of sustained consideration.
>
> (p. 172)

Johnson notes that any integration of AI technology must include careful consideration of the myriad issues attached to AI and must be built on critical digital literacies on the part of the instructor. Citing Stuart Selber, Johnson argues for

> pedagogical innovation that advocates for functional, critical, and rhetorical literacies as a way to prepare students of writing to be effective users, informed questioners, and

DOI: 10.4324/9781003507949-1

> reflective producers of AI and LLM technology "in the service of social action and change."
>
> (pp. 171–172)

As Johnson (2023) argues in his discussion, instructors cannot expect students to use any tool effectively or critically if they are not taught to do so. We argue that there are many reasons Composition instructors should teach students to use AI for writing. We know students are turning to AI tools to complete writing assignments. We also know there is no reliable way to detect when students are using AI tools, and though many writing instructors feel confident they can spot AI-produced writing, the reality is that their detection is unreliable and they tend to overestimate their own accuracy in identifying AI-produced text (Fleckenstein et al., 2023). Consequently, we must acknowledge that writing generated by AI is present in our students' work. We can either abandon them to learn how to use these tools on their own, which will likely mean that the skills they learn are limited to determining how to use AI to produce a passable assignment, or we can teach them how to use AI in ways that are critical and reflective, which will allow them to continue to develop their writing and AI-use skills in ways that will benefit them beyond the classroom.

Additionally, even if methods such as water-marking or text analysis become more reliable in identifying AI-generated language, this would only address the final product – the essay the student turns in. Although this would be important for those who want policies against AI-generated language in academic work, it would have no effect on AI tools augmenting student work at other stages in the writing process. During their May 2024 announcements of new products, both Google and OpenAI gave a nod to the fastest-growing developer focus of 2024 – the building of AI-powered agents that can operate tools for users and perform stages of a more complex task while the user does other things (Google I/O, 2024; OpenAI, 2024). It is not hard to imagine the citation process or research, note-taking, annotation, and outlining processes being farmed out by students to AI agents, and there will be no way for instructors to know which work is human-only, which is AI-only, and which is some combination of human and AI. This is the most likely future of research and writing. It will not be possible to police every stage of the work.

We argue that teaching students how to write with AI is a responsible reaction to how quickly AI tools are achieving ubiquity in our daily lives and professional workflows. And there is no indication that AI tools are going to disappear. Rather, it is likely that AI tools will continue to advance at a breakneck pace and only become further engrained in our personal and working lives. As we so often tell our students, writing is a skill that is needed in every corner of the professional world, and writing effectively is a desirable skill. This will be no less true when AI tools are fully knitted into workplace writing processes. By introducing students to the process of writing with AI and helping them build the habits of mind that will be necessary for them to use AI critically and effectively, we can better prepare them for a future where writing with AI will be expected in many professional settings. We believe that turning away from AI or attempting to outlaw it in our classrooms will do little but leave our students less prepared than other students. We believe that not only does AI have a place in Composition classrooms but instructors also have a responsibility to help students develop AI literacy and begin learning how to use these tools as a part of the composition process.

To that end, this book aims to offer Composition instructors a baseline understanding of how AI tools work, how this technology developed, and how the AI and Composition issue falls into a history of educators' reactions to new technologies. This understanding constitutes a foundation on which instructors may begin to incorporate AI into their Composition classrooms, through either discrete activities and discussions (covered in Chapter 2) or a full integration of AI in the writing process (covered in Chapter 3). Our hope is that whether you are just starting to think about how AI might enter your classroom or you have already welcomed AI into your students' writing processes, this book will offer you useful information on AI and specific strategies and activities you can use to move forward with your incorporation of AI into your writing instruction.

While the authors of this book agree that AI should have a place in the teaching of writing, we have varying approaches to incorporating AI into our classes, and we do not agree on all particulars regarding how AI should be incorporated into Composition instruction now, or what an AI-infused writing curriculum might look like in the future. We believe this diversity of thought is a benefit to this book and to our readers, as we imagine that our readers are more likely to find a compatible voice in the pages of this book due to our different viewpoints.

Here, we introduce ourselves and articulate our individual perspectives on AI and describe the role AI plays in our classrooms.

Dr. Melick views the advent of AI as one instance in a long legacy of technological innovations that have transformed education, and the teaching of writing in particular. While she recognizes that there are fundamental differences between AI LLMs and earlier technological advances, she believes that the best way for Composition instructors to address AI tools – that are present in their classrooms whether they would have them there or not – is to learn about AI tools and their potential for writing, and to help students learn how these tools can be incorporated in meaningful and successful writing processes. Thus far, Dr. Melick has incorporated AI tools into a few assignments in her writing courses; these assignments are designed to guide students through the process of interacting with LLMs for the first time, reflecting on those experiences, and deciding for themselves if and how AI will factor into their writing processes. Dr. Melick does ask students to document if and how AI was used in their writing process for major writing assignments. This requirement allows students to be honest about how the tools were used and how successful students think their use of the tool was. The purpose of this requirement is less to police student use of AI and more to encourage students to think reflectively and critically about how AI benefits (or doesn't) their writing, but it does also serve the purpose of holding students accountable for a type of documentation regarding their AI use.

Dr. Melick's contribution to this book in Chapter 2 offers a few examples of discrete assignments and activities that guide students through using AI tools that can be incorporated into Composition courses. This chapter also offers guidance on how to introduce and discuss the topic of AI with Composition students. The activities and assignments in Chapter 2 are what the authors of this book have been referring to as "toe-dipping exercises" – they offer instructors guidance on how to dip their toes into the waters of AI and Composition if they have not yet begun to integrate AI-supported writing into their courses.

Dr. Plate's position is that creative experimentation and carefree innovation are the best responses to AI. Anxiety and fear will do nothing but hold us back. Dr. Plate's background is in creative writing, and he has spent significant time over the years studying various subfields of computer science and literary movements, such as OuLiPo. He is influenced by poets developing texts with generative AI methods such as Sasha Stiles, David Jhave Johnston, and Allison Parrish and the experimental poetics they pick up and drop as the spirit moves. He has also taught Composition since his first graduate course decades ago, attempting throughout those years to find ways to incorporate experimental approaches to language into the more standard requirements of Composition and first-year writing programs.

Dr. Plate's contributions to this book, especially in Chapter 3, offer an "all-out" approach to integrating AI into the Composition classroom. Students in the classroom described in Chapter 3 are encouraged to use AI for any part of the writing process, from brainstorming to the drafting and revision of full essays. This leads to very different writing processes and very different problem areas in the papers produced by students. For example, a paper submitted by a relatively unskilled student using AI for the writing will have few, if any, grammatical mistakes, but it will suffer from serious problems with generic and vague writing, a shortage of specific examples, and made-up sources. Each of these can be just as problematic – and just as much in need of instruction and professor guidance – as the sentence-level errors that many English professors have spent countless hours correcting. The conceptual discussions that result from using AI to write papers are also quite different, involving rabbit-hole conversations about copyright law and the role of human agency in language and thought.

As outlined later, Chapter 1 will provide a brief historical narrative situating developments of AI of special relevance for Composition instructors and students within broad historical events as well as within the field of Writing Studies. Particular attention is given to the 2023 *Composition Studies* issue referenced earlier as a context for recent scholarship articulating the challenges we face as instructors and our students face as often bewildered users of new technologies while navigating the equally new realities of the university. Differences among us as co-authors of this book are spelled out quite clearly earlier and in our varied pedagogical approaches in Chapters 2 and 3. In Chapter 1, these differences are less overt but still significant. We write this book very much immersed in the same confusion and hectic getting-up-to-speed ambition our colleagues and our students express as they attempt to follow the near-daily news of AI releases and projections. For some, the response has a stronger element of excitement and experimental pleasure; for others, this excitement is tempered by caution and concerns about the responsible, ethical adoption of these tools. There is no way to edit the language of the book until a unified perspective emerges. It seems better to offer a mix of points of view and practical applications and allow the reader to pick and choose.

What should a Composition instructor know when thinking about how to use AI tools in their classroom?

This question assumes a few things. First, it assumes this instructor will be using AI in their classroom. Any question limits the field of possible responses, and our question begins after the branching point of the prior question, "Will I use AI in my classroom?". We assume a "yes" answer and then proceed with the possibilities that result.

Second, that framing question sidesteps the complicated distinction between "artificial intelligence" and "machine learning," opting for the more popular term of the moment (artificial intelligence) and leaving it at that – any reader interested in learning more about this distinction should consult Gallagher (2023) for a discussion of the two terms in relation to Composition and Writing Studies.

Third, the question chooses to imagine a learning space that is not AI-infused within which something we call an "AI tool" is "used." The nature of this assumption is harder to bring out, and we hope its implications will be made clear in Chapter 1. For now, it is enough to say that the classroom we posit does not exist within the AI somehow. The students and the instructor and all the structure of the course can still be encountered without the AI simply by choosing to put AI down or set it aside. A person can choose to write and think with AI and can choose to do so without AI, and that is an assumption we make in this question.

Now, what is a preliminary sketched-out answer to the question?

A Composition instructor should know at least a bit about what a large language model (LLM) is. They should know how to find the AI tools referred to in the question and how to point their students to the tools. They should be aware that these tools are provided by corporations pouring huge amounts of money into their development and actively competing quite fiercely with each other over the adoption and use of these tools. The Composition instructor should also know that the corporations and labs developing AI tools have complex relationships not only with each other as competitors but also with their customers and with the sources of data for this development. And the instructor should be aware that "sources of data" can be very difficult to distinguish from "customers" in the previous sentence. Concepts such as "training," "inference," "intellectual property," and "alignment" should probably take their place next to terms more perennial for Composition instructors such as "equity," "academic integrity," and "bias." A central purpose in Chapter 1 is to outline this information so that an instructor will feel prepared to make informed choices about how to incorporate AI in their Composition courses and what factors they must consider carefully as they invite AI into their classrooms.

Out of this whole mix of things emerges a choice the instructor might make. On the one hand, the instructor might focus on issues of bias and equity and the serious ethical problems implied by thinking of humans as "sources of data." A great deal of sophisticated work in Writing Studies is available for the instructor trying to create safe methods for incorporating AI into their pedagogy. In addition to offering overviews of important AI-related issues and concepts, a good deal of Chapter 1 is devoted to offering a theoretical sketch for such a thoughtful, ethical approach. Chapter 2 offers practical examples of activities that incorporate AI that will further prepare the instructor for implementing this approach in the actual classroom. The activities outlined in Chapter 2 are designed to ease instructors into teaching writing with AI; these assignments primarily help students begin to experiment with AI, learn how to critically evaluate AI output, and reflect on their experiences with AI-supported writing.

Another possible response to the arrival of these tools is to cast a glance toward the disciplines of computer science, certain branches of philosophy, the tradition of experimental poetics within creative writing, and the long history of rhetoric as the basis for experimental composition. This kind of instructor will not ignore the ethical considerations but might be inclined to experiment first and see what happens. This instructor might also question whether a clear dividing line exists between the human author and the machine language generator. Passages in Chapter 1 linger more on the nature of models, analogies between the writer and the model, and speculation about changes in authorship itself might resonate more with this other kind of instructor. And the extended practical example laid out in Chapter 3 will give some food for thought.

Of course, there is no need to choose between the two approaches described in Chapters 2 and 3. One can be curious about organic and non-organic mechanisms for generating language and also voice caution as to misinformation and bias in LLMs. The shape of the book, however, allows a temporary visit first to one approach and then another. We hope the experience is a valuable one.

References

Fleckenstein, J., Meyer, J., Jansen, T., Keller, S., Köller, O., & Möller, J. (2023). Do teachers spot AI? Evaluating the detectability of AI-generated texts among student essays. *Computers and Education: Artificial Intelligence*, *6*, 1–9.

Gallagher, J. R. (2023). Lessons learned from machine learning researchers about the terms "artificial intelligence" and "machine learning." *Composition Studies*, *51*(1), 149–154.

Johnson, G. P. (2023). Don't act like you forgot: Approaching another literacy "crisis" by (re)considering what we know about teaching writing with and through technologies. *Composition Studies*, *51*(1), 169–175.

1 Pedagogical Foundations of AI Integration

Daniel Plate, Elizabeth Melick, and James Hutson

1.1 AI and the Composition Classroom: How Did We Get Here?

The panic and fear inspired by the release of ChatGPT-3 in November 2022 is just one example in a long legacy of negative reactions to new technologies within the context of education and knowledge. At that time, Stephen Marche's (2022) "The College Essay is Dead," in *The Atlantic* provoked extreme reactions from many within the higher education community, and this reaction was particularly noteworthy within fields like Writing Studies, where the "threat" of artificial intelligence large language models (LLMs) seemed especially strong, as the skill many of us have devoted our careers to teaching seemed on the cusp of being automated and irrelevant as a topic of instruction.

While the fear expressed by Composition faculty after the launch of ChatGPT-3 is understandable, this type of response is not new. Throughout human history, leaders and educators have rejected new technologies that seemed poised to revolutionize the ways information was recorded and transmitted. In his *Phaedrus*, Plato (14, 274c-275b) relates how Socrates decried the invention of writing technologies, arguing that writing would lead to forgetfulness and a superficial appearance of wisdom, as people would rely more on written words than their own memory and understanding. Similar fears are often expressed in response to AI tools; many educators lament that the way AI tools make it easy to generate passable writing may very well lead to a new generation of students who are incapable of the kind of critical thinking and close attention required

DOI: 10.4324/9781003507949-2

to plan, draft, revise, and edit a strong piece of argumentative writing.

In spite of the rejections of writing technologies such as Plato's, writing became widely accepted and practiced among educated elites, but when the printing press began to gain popularity in Europe, some people who had previously been wealthy or privileged enough to have access to literacy tried to reject the new technology that would expand access to reading materials considerably. One monk, Johannes Trithemius, wrote a treatise titled *In Praise of Scribes* that advocated for a continued reliance on hand-copying instead of printing. Trithemius cited a perceived poor durability of printed books in contrast to hand-copied manuscripts, also arguing that printed books tended to be of poorer quality and lesser value than hand-copied texts. Trithemius suggested that the labor of copying texts was most appropriate for monks and that resorting to printing amounted to laziness, though it is notable that Trithemius himself elected to circulate his treatise in print to reach a wider audience (Arnold, 1974). In Trithemius' rejection of printing and insistence on the more laborious process of hand-copying, we can see an analog of some of the fears that have surfaced in response to the rise of AI tools, both of which are rooted in a sense of vocation. Trithemius links hand-copying to the vocation of being a monk, and a fear that monks who are not needed for copying books will lack purpose is evident in his treatise. Similarly, many Composition instructors have felt fear that their courses will no longer be needed when writing becomes an automated task, rather than one that requires practice and reflection to hone.

New fears surfaced again in 1801 when chalkboards were introduced to educational settings, as widespread revolts erupted among students and educators who had been trained to memorize (Krause, 2000). In the 1970s, debates were sparked by an increasingly common presence of calculators in math classrooms. The backlash was rooted in fears that students would fail to develop core mathematical competencies if they relied on calculators too often (Werner, 1980). In both cases, we see a rejection of a new tool or technology because educators equated the labor of memorizing or calculating with the skill itself. Time may prove that the rejection of AI tools for writing is similar in kind. Currently, the act of writing word by word is often equated with the skill of being able to write well, though that perception may change as AI becomes more accepted and widely used.

The field of Writing Studies has more recently grappled with increased access to computers and word processors, the internet, and easily accessible online information. In the late 1990s, some leaders in the Composition field charted a path toward embracing new technologies in the Composition classroom, which is evident in texts like Palmquist, Kiefer, Hartvigsen, and Goodlew's *Transitions: Teaching Writing in Computer-Supported and Traditional Classrooms* (1998) and Palmquist and Zimmerman's *Writing with a Computer* (1999). Both of these texts offer similar approaches to the advent of ubiquitous computer usage to the one taken in this book, as they explored potential issues and challenges with the new technology, offered suggestions for how current teaching practices could be adapted to include new technologies, discussed suggestions for using new technologies more effectively, and considered how writing and writing classrooms might be transformed in the future.

Once computer use became an expected aspect of the writing process, increased access to the internet in the early 2000s posed new challenges for Composition instructors. While instructors could previously assume that students would conduct their research through their campus libraries, where all or most discoverable information was already vetted and reliable, new tools like Google and Wikipedia meant that students had access to a great deal of information that was unverified and accessible at their fingertips. Information sourced from Wikipedia and Google was unwelcome in academic writing, and articles like Carr's (2008) "Is Google Making Us Stupid?" did little to assuage fears that the internet was a detriment to knowledge and intellect in general. Over time, our field has generally come to acknowledge the value that these non-academic tools can provide to the academic writing process. The popular Composition

OER text *Writing Spaces* has even included several essays that reframe the Google and Wikipedia debate, such as Purdy's "Wikipedia is Good for You!?" (2010) and McClure's "Googlepedia: Turning Information Behaviors into Research Skills" (2011), which help students to understand the role these tools can play in their research and writing process.

In each of these cases, initial fear and revulsion eventually gave way to widespread acceptance of the new technology, along with related progress in human thought and achievement that was bolstered by common implementation of the new tool. Similarly, the initial resistance to AI from educators is gradually giving way to an acknowledgment of its potential benefits. Many educators, including those who teach Composition and writing courses, are increasingly focusing on how AI can augment writing processes and support stronger writing in students, rather than eliminating the need for students to learn how to write well. Still, many educators, including many Composition faculty, remain resistant to the inclusion of AI in college classrooms, pointing to many legitimate concerns with the tools that are discussed at the conclusion of this section.

We argue that AI does have a place in Composition classrooms, and just as students learned to write, rather than memorize, or print, rather than copy by hand, our students will also learn to incorporate these new technologies into their work in a beneficial way. Still, it is important to acknowledge that the comparison of AI to previous "disruptive" technologies has its limit. Unlike writing, printing, and word processors, AI LLMs go further than making it easier to record and transmit human thought. Instead, LLMs can produce ideas and text, which do constitute a fundamental departure from the nature of previous new technologies that have had strong effects on education. This distinction is critical in understanding the implications AI has in shaping the future of writing and education, highlighting a shift from simple technological aid to a collaborator in the creative and intellectual processes. AI tools are certainly distinct in nature from previous technological advances. However, we still maintain it is important that AI is present in college classrooms, including writing classrooms, and that a purposeful approach to these new tools can help our field grow, rather than diminish, and help our students flourish as communicators and writers, rather than disregard writing skills as irrelevant. We argue that increased use of AI will make the skills that our courses teach, such as critical thinking, creativity, and problem-solving skills, even more important as they will distinguish students with those habits of mind in the classroom and the workplace as AI is increasingly relied on for routine tasks (Wilson, 2001; Autor & Dorn, 2013; Frey & Osborne, 2017).

As we consider how AI might be integrated in Composition courses and anticipate that it will have a profound effect on our field, we can look back at the seismic shifts brought about by the Agricultural, Industrial, and Information Revolutions. All of these transformative periods were initiated by innovation but were also marked by significant disruption to previous ways of life. For instance, during the Agricultural Revolution that occurred around 10,000 BCE, the shift from nomadic hunter-gatherer societies to agriculture-based communities fostered the growth of large permanent settlements, which led to the development of specialized roles and skills within society (Kerridge, 2013). The invention of writing in Mesopotamia circa 3400 BCE revolutionized communication, enabling the transmission of knowledge across generations. The Industrial Revolution in the late 18th and early 19th centuries further disrupted societies as their citizens transitioned from rural agrarian lifestyles to urban industrialization (Deane, 1979). The era demanded adaptation to new work environments, such as factories, and heralded the growth of urban centers, though these shifts in work styles, locations, and environments led to a poor quality of life for many. Subsequently, the Information Age, characterized by the proliferation of computers and the internet, transformed the global economy from industrial to knowledge-based (Castells, 2009). The period saw a rise in digital professions, a decline in manual labor, and the onset of automation.

The 2010s marked the advent of the Internet of Things (IoT), heralding an era when physical devices, vehicles, and appliances became interconnected and capable of exchanging data, thus creating intelligent, responsive systems (Minoli, 2013). These new links between physical and digital domains led to a significant leap in the way humans interact with both their environment and technology (Zanella et al., 2014). During this Third Industrial Revolution and the age of the Internet of Things, technology has become integrated into most aspects of everyday life and work, which set the stage for the next leap in interaction between humans and technology: the integration of AI tools in many areas of our professional and personal lives.

This current age, called Industry 4.0 by many, is driven by AI and the Internet of Things (IoT). In this age, physical and digital integration will soon incorporate biological systems as well, marking a new chapter in history (Schwab, 2017). As technology and AI become further engrained in our daily lives – and perhaps even our minds and bodies – there will be an increasing need for the adaptable skills taught in Composition classrooms, where critical thinking, creativity, and problem-solving are emphasized. These skills are essential for navigating the challenges and opportunities of a technology-driven world, where understanding diverse cultures and perspectives is crucial for global engagement (Crossley & Tikly, 2004). As we step forward into this new age, we may see certain types of jobs become obsolete, though we can be confident that new ones will emerge as they always have during ages of major advancements in forms of work. This new age and the changes it will bring will require a continual process of learning and adaptation. The Fourth Industrial Revolution represents not just a technological advancement but a call to reimagine and retool for a future that blends human ingenuity with technological advancements. By inviting AI into our Composition classrooms, we can help our students build the skills that will help them adapt to the rapid change these new technologies will undoubtedly bring to the landscape of work in the near and distant future.

The 2023 special issue of *Composition Studies* offers a corrective to some aspects of this historical sketch. One of the issues addressed by multiple authors in the issue is the potential for AI technologies, including writing tools, to perpetuate and amplify biases and inequities. Both Antonio Byrd and Alfred L. Owusu-Ansah call attention to the ways in which the corpus texts used to train LLMs, often sourced from the internet without regard for representational issues, encode the linguistic patterns, and value judgments of dominant groups while erasing or misrepresenting marginalized voices and non-standard language practices. As AI tools are increasingly deployed in educational and professional contexts, Composition scholars and instructors in the classroom have a responsibility to push for more inclusive and equitable practices.

Several articles in the 2023 issue point to the importance of drawing on the field's existing theoretical frameworks and pedagogical approaches to develop productive strategies for integrating AI into writing instruction. S. Scott Graham makes the case for using post-process theories of writing, which emphasize the situated and recursive nature of composing, to help students engage with AI tools as part of a larger writing ecology. Similarly, Courtney Stanton advocates for "Writing about Writing" pedagogies, which teach students disciplinary knowledge about writing and rhetoric, to empower them to analyze and critique the affordances and limitations of AI tools. These perspectives suggest that rather than viewing AI as a threat to replace writing instruction, the field should proactively adapt its teaching to help students navigate an increasingly AI-mediated writing landscape.

Many of these articles argue for critical and ethical consideration by scholars who decide to use AI in their work and classrooms. As several articles note, both the source data that are used to train AI tools and the AI corporations themselves are often dominated by privileged voices and language. Annette Vee argues that the field should resist the tendency to view writing solely in terms of the production of error-free, standardized texts and instead reaffirm the value of writing as a mode of inquiry, learning, and personal growth – all qualities that current AI tools struggle to emulate. Already mentioned earlier, Gavin P. Johnson draws on the field's history of engaging with other digital technologies to spell out the four tenets described earlier, especially the need to attend to the ethical dimensions of technology use and give students hands-on opportunities to experiment and reflect on their writing even as writing practices change.

The special issue is a glimpse into a subfield that is still in the early stages of processing the implications of AI writing tools but that is committed to shaping the role that these technologies will play in the teaching of writing. The authors express varying degrees of optimism and concern about the future of writing under the pressure of such outsized influence by corporate-backed and delivered tools. All of the authors push for a future that is more inclusive and ethical. As such, the special issue represents an important early contribution to an ongoing and evolving conversation. The contributions to this special issue also offer a strong representation of varying perspectives from within the field, and considered together, these articles comprise a convenient primer on the most relevant AI-related topics in the field of Composition. Though the authors of the articles included in the *Composition Studies* issue on AI do not present uniform approaches to AI, the issue as a whole demonstrates that continued discussion of how AI might be incorporated into Composition curricula is warranted.

1.2 AI Literacy: What Instructors Need to Know?

In a May 8, 2020, interview, the AI scientist, Ilya Sutskever (then working at OpenAI), was asked what he considered the most "beautiful or surprising idea in deep learning or AI in general" (Fridman, 2020, 29:40). Sutskever responded, "The most beautiful thing about deep learning is that it actually works" (Fridman, 29:48). Sutskever then followed up, "And now we just train these neural networks and you make them larger and they keep getting better, and I find it unbelievable" (Fridman, 30:12–30:16). This was in 2020, when GPT-2 was state-of-the-art. Since then, companies like Anthropic, Google, Meta, and OpenAI have continued to train neural networks, continued throwing more and more data at the models, continued making them larger and larger, and they continue to get better. Any graph of resources put into compute for AI and the size of the resulting models will show almost a flatline up until around 2020 and then start on an exponential curve that shows, at the time of this book in May of 2024, no sign of flattening.

What does this mean for Composition instructors? Probably the most important reality for instructors is the same thing Sutskever gives as his answer: These tools actually work. Coming on the heels of the crash of FTX and other cryptocurrencies, the announcement of ChatGPT-3 in late November 2022 could have been seen as one more example of tech shysters hyping up their products. But by December 6, 2022, Stephen Marche was making clear in "The College Essay is Dead" the crucial point. This tech works. It's not simply a future-focused dream. It can already write a college essay. It is time for scholars and instructors of Composition to give themselves more context for what's to come and for what's already here.

Most simply put, ChatGPT (or Anthropic's chatbot Claude or Google's Gemini) is a chatbot user interface (UI) that allows humans to interact with a large language model (LLM). ChatGPT is not the LLM itself. The LLM Ilya Sutskever described previously was named GPT-2, and it had no easy UI for customers to use. The next model, GPT-3, also had no widely used UI for months (see, however, Chapter 3 for an example of students using the GPT-3 Playground prior to the release of ChatGPT-3). It was the recasting of the LLM through a chatbot UI that led to the (seemingly) instant take-off of this technology. Current demonstrations of AI models in May 2024 speculate about interacting with AI through glasses, through fluid audio exchanges with phones, and more. These demos are about the UI. Underneath are the models.

The question of what an LLM is begins with what a model is. We use models to understand complex aspects or parts of reality by constructing simplified or abstracted versions of reality, or at least of those parts of reality we are studying. Part of understanding something through a model is attempting to predict its likely behavior. A model of domestic cat behavior will attempt to predict circumstances in which a sequence of behavior common in all cats (domestic or not) might differ in a cat used to living with humans. A model of language typically used in academic writing in our discipline would attempt to predict whether the sequence

"A Shakespearean sonnet typically ends with ________"

will more likely continue with the words "a couplet" or "two strings of characters with a carriage return between them."

The history of modeling language using machines has largely taken place in computer science. The first sophisticated language models have been called statistical language models (SLMs), an approach to the machine modeling of language begun in the 1980s and reaching greater effectiveness in the 1990s. These models could make predictions based on fixed sequences of words but could not make predictions very far into the sentence or the wider text. SLMs were followed by neural language models (NLMs) in the 2000s and 2010s and then eventually by pre-trained language models (PLMs) in the later 2010s. Examples of PLMs included BERT, introduced by Google in 2018, and GPT-2, created by OpenAI and released in 2019. The large language model (LLM) is a kind of PLM that has been trained on a very large amount of data; typically, an LLM is described in terms of the scale of the model's parameters. Parameters can be described as the elements within the model that can adjust or that can learn or change during the process of training the model on very large data sets. Both GPT-2 and GPT-3 are pre-trained language models, which explain why their knowledge base is fixed and limited by the date of the conclusion of their period of training. The difference between GPT-2 and GPT-3 is one of scale, with GPT-2 having 1.5 billion parameters and GPT-3 coming in at 175 billion parameters (Zhao et al., 2023, pp. 1–3).

The remarkable surprise of these LLMs is the variety of emergent capabilities that show up as the scale of the training gets much, much larger. Sometimes referred to as "the bitter lesson," based on a 2019 essay of that name by AI researcher Richard

Sutton, it seems to be the case that the most effective way of adding capabilities to these models comes more from simply scaling up the size and complexity of the data ("brute-forcing" things) than from trying to instill human knowledge into the model or using human ingenuity to build the systems. This observation of Sutton is related to two ongoing trends in AI technology. The first is the frequency of comments like Sutskever's – said almost with a shrug – that more and more data will be added to the systems until this fails to continue accelerating the trend of improvement. The second trend is toward increasing speed of processing and response in chatbots like ChatGPT. The term for this is "inference," which is the user's input of a prompt and the output of some response, as opposed to "training," which is the development of the model from all the data gathered from wherever the companies have found it. This increasing speed of inference has been accompanied during 2023 and 2024 by a reduction in user cost, especially at the application programming interface (API) layer of the model. These are generally website interfaces made available by OpenAI, Google, or Anthropic to developers who want to access the models using code, rather than a user-friendly UI.

In May of 2024, OpenAI announced that their new GPT-4o (GPT-Omni) model would be freely available soon to worldwide users. If this promise becomes a reality, and if other companies follow suit in order to compete for users, this might address important cost and equity concerns of Composition instructors attempting to use AI tools in the classroom. A very early concern about the use of AI tools in educational settings was related to the cost and tiered subscription services; namely, if an AI tool's paid subscription offers significantly better outputs than the free model does, this could create inequity among students if some can afford the subscription costs while others cannot. If companies like OpenAI decide that making state-of-the-art models available for free serves their interests as well as those of the user, the divide between students who can afford to pay subscription costs for the best models and students who cannot afford it may be less serious than it has been so far. This remains to be seen, however.

It has become almost common knowledge that all an LLM does is predict the next word in a sequence. This shorthand definition will sometimes have a tone of awe at how much ChatGPT can do by simply predicting the next word, and it will sometimes have the deflationary tone of a figure like Emily Bender or Gary Marcus in his current-paths-in-AI-skeptical book *Rebooting AI: Building Artificial Intelligence We Can Trust*. While LLM outputs can be impressive (though, as many have noted, the language produced in response to basic prompts tends to be generic and lifeless), according to this more deflationary account, the LLM has no understanding of what it is producing. LLMs are trained on vast amounts of data that help them predict the most likely response a user is looking for based on the prompt submitted. As Aimée Morrison (2023) explains, LLMs are "programmed to calculate plausible-sounding (not 'correct,' please note) text output in response to a prompt" (p. 157). LLMs are making well-informed guesses based on vast amounts of data, but they do not understand what they are producing in the same way that humans do.

The fact that LLMs are trained on human data, which inevitably include the biases that humans hold, can lead to issues with LLM outputs. As Antonio Byrd (2023) explains, LLMs "learn a form of language, but do not understand the implicit meaning behind it" (p. 136), and their lack of understanding of context for the text they generate can cause harm. A further associated issue is that the data sets used to train LLMs are often poor representations of varied viewpoints, perspectives, experiences, and literacies, meaning that people with marginalized identities may be underrepresented in the LLM's training. All these factors can lead to LLMs producing biased writing that reflects the biases of the humans who produced the texts they were trained on and the humans who chose the data sets used to train the LLM.

Yet another layer of bias is created by the companies who operate LLMs, who often add "guardrails" to their LLMs to try to prevent their tools from producing harmful content. In many cases, these guardrails are beneficial as they prevent LLMs from producing text that may cause harm for users. However, there have already been many documented cases of AI companies' guardrails working poorly or producing a different set of biases in which LLMs refuse to produce texts that take conservative stances on hot-button issues or refuse to take stances at all. The question of the "bias in the machine" is an important one that reinforces the necessity for an approach to AI that is grounded in the concepts and theories that have long formed the foundation for Composition instruction. We know that AI tools will demonstrate biases, but we also know that no text that has ever been produced has been free from bias. Teaching our students to approach AI-produced writing and writing with AI with the same critical analysis and rhetorical awareness that we teach our students to use for all texts will prepare them to be successful and well-informed writers whether or not AI is part of their writing process.

That the LLM is trying to produce a likely or plausible response for users offers a partial explanation for why AI-generated writing is often described as formally and grammatically correct (according to the rules of Standard American English) but bland. LLMs' programming aims for "likely" and "plausible," which tends to drive the writing it generates toward the middle in every way, as it produces generally amenable prose that avoids taking strong stances. Morrison (2023) (quoting Emily Bender and Timnit Gebru) dismisses AI writing as "an imitation game . . . a stochastic parrot" (p. 160). This highlights an issue that instructors must address when teaching students how to use AI tools: How to maintain their unique voice in their AI-infused/assisted writing and avoid the dull, flat language that LLMs tend to produce without additional prompting. Some of our students have even noted that LLMs' word choice and sentence structures are not ones that they would ever choose for themselves. This is an area where purposeful instruction in writing with AI is necessary: Students must be told that they can use their prompts and revision processes to use AI to write in a voice and tone that is suitable for them and an accurate reflection of both what they want to say and how they want to say it.

Another issue related to writing with AI (and indeed all generative AI tools) is the question of intellectual property. Some have objected to the practices used to train LLMs, in which data were pulled from publicly available text on the internet and fed into the LLMs as samples. Though the text included in these data sets was publicly available (in theory – as Byrd (2023) notes, OpenAI, the creators of ChatGPT, do not offer access to their corpus texts and admit that some of their data set was sourced from third-party providers), there have been many objections to the use of these texts for the training of LLMs as a potential breach of intellectual property (IP) rights.

The IP debate does not end with the concern of the data on which LLMs were trained, however; the question of who "owns" the IP produced by LLMs has also posed significant issues for AI companies and writers who use AI. The case of Kristina Kashtanova's partially AI-generated graphic novel *Zarya of the Dawn* highlights some of the complex IP issues surrounding works created with the assistance of AI. In September 2022, Kashtanova obtained copyright registration for the novel from the U.S. Copyright Office. However, the Office later initiated a cancellation of the registration after discovering that Kashtanova had used Midjourney, an AI image generation tool, to create some of the artwork (US Copyright Office, 2023, p. 2).

The Copyright Office took issue with the fact that Kashtanova's copyright application had not disclosed the use of AI and claimed her as the sole author. They argued that the portions of the work generated by Midjourney lacked sufficient human authorship to qualify for copyright protection. In their decision, the Office drew a distinction between an artist using AI as a tool guided by their own creative vision versus the AI generating images autonomously in a way the artist does not control or predict. They held that "A person who provides text prompts to Midjourney does not 'actually form' the generated images and is not the 'master mind' behind them" (US Copyright Office, 2023, p. 9). The individual AI-generated images in Kashtanova's work fell into the latter category and could not be copyrighted.

However, the Office did affirm that the parts of the work that were clearly Kashtanova's own creation, including the written story, the selection and arrangement of the AI images, and the overall design of the graphic novel, met the threshold of originality required for copyright. So while they denied protection for the individual AI-generated images, they issued a new copyright registration covering the other creative elements Kashtanova contributed. The case illustrates how current copyright law, which requires human authorship for protection, is grappling with works that have both human-authored and autonomously machine-generated components. It suggests that the more an artist guides, curates, and integrates AI-generated content into their overall creative vision, the more likely the work as a whole will qualify for some amount of copyright protection, even if the AI portions on their own do not. However, the dividing line remains murky. As generative AI tools become more widely used by artists and writers, cases like Kashtanova's will continue to spur debate about how intellectual property frameworks should evolve to accommodate human-AI collaborations.

As this last more extended example shows, the nature of authorship itself will need redefinition as human-AI hybrid work enters the public sphere, including the semi-public sphere of the Composition classroom. Each of the concerns from this section will both require critical engagement and provide new opportunities for intellectual growth.

1.3 The Student Writer in the AI Classroom: Reflections on Voice, Authorship, and Authority

Examples abound of panic about the consequences of AI disruption. One of these is the worry about deep fakes, images, and misinformation. If AI tools can be used to alter existing images or create plausible images from scratch of things that did not actually happen, what will this do to our understanding of the world and of our ability to depend on the news or what we read or watch on the internet? In Cade Metz's popular history of recent AI scientists, *Genius Makers: The Mavericks Who Brought AI to Google, Facebook, and the World*, Ian Goodfellow has this to say about the implications of AI-generated images: "These [methods of generating images] would end the era where images were proof that something had happened. It's been a little bit of a fluke, historically, that we're able to rely on videos as evidence that something really happened" (Metz, 2021). As one of the primary developers of an image-generating technique called generative adversarial networks (GANs), Goodfellow has an interesting vantage point on images.

And it is a profound observation. The fact that we now feel the ground shifting under our feet when it comes to trusting images on the news or on the internet can be interpreted as an opportunity, rather than a disaster. Perhaps we have been trapped by a "fluke" of historical contingency, by the small window of history during which the technology of the camera makes the image a stable record of "what happened." The fact that a new set of technologies destabilizes the photograph is not the disruption of thousands of years of truth – it is a much more local phenomenon, historically speaking. Maybe we shouldn't have put so much faith in the photograph to begin with. Goodfellow continues,

> We used to actually have to think through a story . . . about who said what and who has the incentive to say what, who has credibility on which issue, and it seems like we're headed back towards those kinds of times.
>
> (Metz, 2021)

This is an argument in favor of critical thinking. Instead of simply accepting video footage and photograph documentation as objective truth, we should be questioning the incentives behind the apparent objectivity of every story, whether supported by an "objective" reality like video/image or not. AI technology simply returns us to what we never should have forgotten, the necessity of critical thinking in evaluating everything we read (or watch). Another historical contingency could be pushed on here as well, one closer to Composition and our students: the historical contingency of word-by-word writing. We have had word-by-word writing for much longer than we have had images (or video). But word-by-word writing is also a technological development. And perhaps AI writing tools are giving us an opportunity to discover what happens when a person can write without typing out the words one at a time.

In Chapter 3 of the present work, a distinction will be made between what we call "higher" and "lower" levels of thought. The words "higher" and "lower" come from computer science, where "lower" refers to instructions that are closer to the machine code and "higher" refers to human-readable code or even pseudocode (code in a concise natural language). A comparison of coding and writing reveals striking parallels in how individuals develop proficiency and sophistication in both. In coding, higher-level concepts revolve around abstraction, utilizing advanced tools, and focusing on overall design and architecture. Similarly, in writing, higher-level skills involve shaping the structure of a piece, developing arguments, and refining the final product. Both domains require a skilled practitioner to go back and forth between the "word-by-word" level of lines of code or sentences and the grouping structures of code (functions or files) and written language (paragraphs and sections of essays).

In the realm of coding, higher-level programming involves working with abstractions that simplify complex tasks. Developers use high-level languages like Python or JavaScript, which abstract away many low-level details such as memory management and hardware interactions. This allows them to concentrate on designing their programs without getting bogged down by intricate technicalities. Libraries and frameworks further exemplify this approach, providing pre-built functionalities that accelerate development and reduce the need to reinvent the wheel.

Lower-level coding demands a detailed understanding of the underlying hardware and system operations. Writing code in languages like C or assembly requires managing memory directly, optimizing performance, and handling system resources meticulously. This level of coding emphasizes fundamental operations and algorithms, necessitating a deep comprehension of how software interacts with hardware. Developers working at this level focus on performance optimization and precise control over the software's behavior.

Similarly, in writing, higher-level skills are concerned with the larger structure and thematic development of the essay or paper. Writers focus on organizing their ideas into coherent sections, figuring out the shape of a narrative, and thinking through the argument-objection-response pattern of an argumentative paper. They might use AI tools to generate initial drafts or provide suggestions, allowing them to concentrate on the structure and flow of thought, rather than matters of grammar, usage, and style. This approach mirrors higher-level coding, where the emphasis is on design and overall logic, rather than detailed implementation.

Lower-level writing, on the other hand, involves careful attention to the actual words at the sentence and paragraph levels. Writers work on constructing clear, grammatically correct sentences, choosing proper punctuation, and making individual word choices. Up until now, this foundational work has been an essential stage of building strong writing skills, just as understanding basic coding operations has been crucial for becoming a proficient programmer. Manual drafting and careful editing are akin to lower-level coding practices, emphasizing the mechanics of language and clarity of expression.

In recent years, however, AI tools have become capable of the low-level work. The first sign of the generative power of AI was not an image generator or ChatGPT. It was an AI coding tool called GitHub Copilot that amazed developers with its ability to generate code at the "word by word" level without coders typing everything out. The debates among developers about whether this makes for better, more efficient coders or coders who will forget how to code mirror the emerging debates in English departments about whether students without strong sentence-level writing skills can benefit from learning to put papers together "one or two levels up" from the sentence.

What is a model? A model is something that simplifies or abstracts in order to aid in tasks of prediction. The kind of prediction one performs with a model might be highly quantitative and precise, but it might not. In "Inventing the University," David Bartholomae (1986) does not use the technical language of financial or meteorological models, but in the evocative opening sentence of his essay, Bartholomae could be describing something like a model: "Every time a student sits down to write for us, he has to invent the university for the occasion" (p. 4). The essay goes on to describe the challenges the student faces in approximating the discourse of this strange new world, the academic institution: "They have to invent the university by assembling and mimicking its language, finding some compromise between idiosyncracy, a personal history, and the requirements of convention, the history of a discipline" (p. 5).

But does this analogy or comparison of the human student with the conceptual model break down right away? Can we allow a comparison between the real human student in the real classroom, feeling the hesitations and insecurities of a first-generation college student, and some non-human thing we sum up with the mathematical or theoretical term "model" and all the cerebral and literal machinery wrapped up in that term? A careful reader of this chapter might bring Emily Bender and Timnit Gebru back with their "stochastic parrot" picture of the LLM and ask directly with some incredulity, "Is the student being framed here as an LLM?" This careful reader might also know that a different voice from this chapter, the AI scientist Ilya Sutskever, would approve of the comparison. For Sutskever, the AI that learned to play Go, AlphaGo, should be described as reasoning. Sutskever argued that the success of AlphaGo and AlphaZero in playing Go at a level "better than 99.9 of all humans" provides "an existence proof that neural networks can reason" (Fridman, 2020, 42:51–43:14).

There is a real tension among the thinkers featured here. Some would find in the language of "pretending" and "mimicking" to describe the student a very fruitful and exciting overlap with what LLMs seem to be doing. Many others would object and object quite strenuously. The human student does something very different when taking those first steps in pretending to be a college student than what the LLM does when prompted to "pretend to be a freshman Composition student and write a draft of an essay." This chapter does not have the space or scope for addressing this tension in any thorough way. We simply observe this variety of perspectives and attempt a picture of what we might be doing as we bring AI into the classroom.

Bartholomae (1986) reflects in his essay on the privilege of the academic insider who can use the language of the university with confidence and authority and encourages the Composition instructor to think carefully about what it means to "pretend" to be a college writer and to invent the whole thing from the ground up. His essay helps us think about how AI writing tools can support students in learning to write within academic communities. Just as Bartholomae describes students needing to "appropriate" the specialized language of the university, AI can serve as a scaffolding to help students approximate the conventions and styles of academic writing, even before they have fully mastered these skills on their own. Bartholomae's argument that students must "mimic" the language of the new academic setting they find themselves in and find "some compromise" between their own voice and the voices and "history of a discipline" can be reinterpreted as a fruitful analogy for what a student writer might do in writing in collaboration with an AI (p. 5). This act of invention is a step in students' development as academic writers, and it is not an easy step. Students "have to do this as though they were easily and comfortably one with their audience, as though they were members of the academy" (pp. 4–5), even though they are still learning the ropes.

Here is where AI writing tools can have a role. By generating suggestions and drafts in response to students' prompts, AI can help students experiment with the language and conventions of academic writing in a low-stakes environment. Students can see how their ideas might be expressed using the specialized vocabulary and rhetorical moves of a particular discipline, without needing to have already mastered these elements themselves. In this way, AI can make the process of "assembling and mimicking" the university's language more accessible and less intimidating for novice writers.

Of course, this process of imitation is not a simple matter of copying or regurgitating the language of the academy. It involves a negotiation between the student's voice and the conventions of the discourse community they are entering. "The writer must get inside of a discourse he can only partially imagine. The act of constructing a sentence, then, becomes something like an act of transcription, where the voice on the tape unexpectedly fades away and becomes inaudible" (p. 19). AI can also serve as a "voice on the tape" for students to transcribe and adapt as they find their own place within the academic discourse. By providing a starting point and a model to work from, AI can help students bridge the gap between their personal language and the expectations of the university. At the same time, AI cannot replace the hard work of "getting inside" the discourse and making it one's own. Students must still figure out how to inhabit the ideas, the arguments, and the rhetorical strategies that make up the substance of academic writing.

Bartholomae's (1986) essay also points to the ways in which the process of learning to write in an academic context is tied to issues of power and identity. He argues that "all writers, in order to write, must imagine for themselves the privilege of being 'insiders' – that is, of being both inside an established and powerful discourse and of being granted a special right to speak" (p. 10). For many students, particularly those from marginalized backgrounds, this can be a difficult and fraught process. They may feel they are being asked to abandon their language and identity to conform to the academy's norms. AI writing tools have the potential to mitigate some of these concerns. By giving students a way to experiment with academic language and conventions without the high stakes of a graded assignment, AI can create a space for students to play with different identities and voices. Students can use AI to help them "try on" the language of the university, seeing how it fits and where it rubs against their own sense of self. In doing so, they may find it easier to locate themselves within the discourse and to claim the "special right to speak" (p. 10).

It's important that the use of AI in the writing classroom does not reinforce existing power imbalances. As Bartholomae describes it,

> the movement toward a more specialized discourse begins (or perhaps, best begins) when a student can both define a position of privilege, a position that sets him against a 'common' discourse, and when he can work self-consciously, critically, against not only the 'common' code but his own. (p. 17)

In other words, the goal is not simply for students to mimic the language of the university but to develop a critical awareness of how that language operates and to find ways to make it their own.

Used in isolation, an AI risks becoming just another way for students to reproduce the language of the academy without fully understanding or interrogating it. Used in the context of a pedagogy that emphasizes critical reflection, however, AI can be a means of helping students to "dare to speak" (p. 5) in their own voices, even as they are learning to navigate the strange and often alienating environments of academic discourse. The goal of writing instruction is not simply to induct students into the university's "set of specifically acceptable gestures and commonplaces" (p. 11), but to empower them to participate in and shape the ongoing conversation of the academy. Used critically and in service of this larger goal, an AI can be a valuable tool in this process. It can help students to find their way into the discourse, to experiment with new ways of writing and thinking, and, ultimately, to claim their own space within the ongoing conversations of the university.

References

Arnold, K. (Ed.). (1974). *In praise of scribes (De Laude Scriptorum)*. Coronado Press.

Autor, D., & Dorn, D. (2013). The growth of low-skill service jobs and the polarization of the US labor market. *American Economic Review*, *103*(5), 1553–1597. https://doi.org/10.1257/aer.103.5.1553

Bartholomae, D. (1986). Inventing the university. *Journal of Basic Writing*, *5*(1), 4–23. https://doi.org/10.37514/JBW-J.1986.5.1.02

Byrd, A. (2023). Truth-telling: Critical inquiries on LLMs and the corpus texts that train them. *Composition Studies*, *51*(1), 135–142.

Carr, N. (2008). Is Google making us stupid? *Teachers College Record*, *110*(14), 89–94.

Castells, M. (2009). *The rise of the network society*. Wiley-Blackwell. https://doi.org/10.1002/9781444319514

Crossley, M., & Tikly, L. (2004). Postcolonial perspectives and comparative and international research in education: A critical introduction. *Comparative Education*, *40*(2), 147–156. https://doi.org/10.1080/0305006042000231347

Deane, P. M. (1979). *The first industrial revolution*. Cambridge University Press.

Frey, C. B., & Osborne, M. A. (2017). The future of employment: How susceptible are jobs to computerisation? *Technological Forecasting and Social Change*, *114*, 254–280. https://doi.org/10.1016/j.techfore.2016.08.019

Fridman, L. (2020, May 8). Ilya Sutskever: Deep learning [Audio podcast episode]. In *Lex Fridman podcast*. www.youtube.com/watch?v=13CZPWmke6A

Kerridge, E. (2013). *The agricultural revolution*. Routledge. https://doi.org/10.4324/9781315019888

Krause, S. D. (2000). "Among the greatest benefactors of mankind": What the success of chalkboards tells us about the future of computers in the classroom. *The Journal of the Midwest Modern Language Association*, *33*(2), 6–16. https://doi.org/10.2307/1315198

Marche, S. (2022, December 6). The college essay is dead. *The Atlantic*. www.theatlantic.com/technology/archive/2022/12/chatgpt-ai-writing-college-student-essays/672371/

Marcus, Gary. (2019). *Rebooting AI: Building artificial intelligence we can trust*. Pantheon.

McClure, R. (2011). Googlepedia: Turning information behaviors into research skills. In C. Lowe & P. Zemliansky (Eds.), *Writing spaces: Readings on writing* (Vol. 2, pp. 221–241). Parlor Press.

Minoli, D. (2013). *Building the internet of things with IPv6 and MIPv6: The evolving world of M2M communications*. John Wiley & Sons.

Morrison, A. (2023). Meta-writing: AI and writing. *Composition Studies*, *51*(1), 155–161.

Palmquist, M., Kiefer, K., Hartvigsen, J., & Goodlew, B. (1998). *Transitions: Teaching writing in computer-supported and traditional classrooms*. Ablex Publishing.

Palmquist, M., & Zimmerman, D. E. (1999). *Writing with a computer*. Allyn and Bacon.

Purdy, J. P. (2010). Wikipedia is good for you!? In C. Lowe & P. Zemliansky (Eds.), *Writing spaces: Readings on writing* (Vol. 1, pp. 205–224). Parlor Press.

Schwab, K. (2017). *The fourth industrial revolution*. Crown Currency.

U.S. Copyright Office. (2023, February 21). *Re: Zarya of the dawn (Registration # VAu001480196)*. https://fingfx.thomsonreuters.com/gfx/legaldocs/klpygnkyrpg/AI%20COPYRIGHT%20decision.pdf

Werner, M. (1980). The hand-held calculator and its impact on mathematics curricula. *School Science and Mathematics*, *80*(1), 29–36.

Wilson, S. (2001). *Information arts: Intersections of art, science, and technology*. The MIT Press. https://doi.org/10.7551/mitpress/3765.001.0001

Zanella, A., Bui, N., Castellani, A., Vangelista, L., & Zorzi, M. (2014). Internet of things for smart cities. *IEEE Internet of Things Journal*, *1*(1), 22–32. https://doi.org/10.1109/JIOT.2014.2306328

Zhao, W. X., Zhou, K., Li, J., Li, T., Wang, X., Hou, Y., Min, Y., Zhang, B., Zhang, J., Dong, Z., Du, Y., Chen, C., Chen, Y., Chen, Y., Nie, Z., Ren, R., Li, Y., Tang, X., Liu, Z., . . . Wen, J. R. (2023). *A survey of large language models*. arXiv preprint. https://arxiv.org/pdf/2303.18223

2 Inviting AI Into the Composition Classroom

Elizabeth Melick and Susan Edele

For many composition instructors, and indeed many members of the broader higher education community, the most significant barrier to using and teaching with AI is the sheer crushing volume of information about AI tools and the ever-increasing number of AI tool options. It is an intimidating prospect to wade through the amount of information and options available in order to identify the best way to introduce AI to a class. Many of the discussions about AI available also come from advanced practitioners who have thoroughly infused AI into their courses (like Daniel Plate, who discusses an AI-infused approach to teaching Composition in Chapter 3). While we acknowledge that these advanced AI instructors are charting a path that many of us will follow as AI becomes more ubiquitous in our work and teaching spaces, we also acknowledge that it is daunting to approach the task of teaching with AI if one believes that the only option is a total infusion of the tools into their courses.

If you are relatively new to using or teaching with AI, we hope this chapter will offer you some ideas for how you can begin to integrate the use of AI into your Composition courses. Here, we offer just a few examples of activities that we have used in our classes to introduce students to AI and help them consider how AI might factor into their writing processes. We argue that any introduction of AI in class ought to be preceded by a meaningful discussion of what AI tools are, how they work, and what factors students need to consider when contemplating the use of an AI tool. We believe that it is also essential for students' first forays into writing with AI to include reflection

DOI: 10.4324/9781003507949-3

and critical analysis, which will help students build a practice of carefully evaluating AI outputs and purposefully considering how well the output matches what they wanted to say. This will help students become effective users of AI tools.

The activities described in this chapter may or may not fit well with how your Composition courses are designed. If they do fit well, we encourage you to use them however you see fit. Even if they don't fit well with your courses, we hope you will use these examples to generate your own ideas for introducing AI. We've also included descriptions of how we present these activities and how our students have responded. We hope that this information will help you anticipate what you might expect when bringing AI into your classrooms, though it is important to acknowledge that your student population may respond differently than ours have, and there can be a great variety in responses, even among classes taught at a single institution.

We offer one final suggestion before we move on to describing our activities: Make sure you have a recommended or required AI tool for students to use for these activities. It should be a tool that offers a free account. Make sure you have created a free account with the tool. If the account set up requires a few steps or verification, you might assign that task to students before the class session in which the AI activity will be completed. You should also practice the activity yourself before you lead the activity in your class; it can be helpful to show students your sample conversation with the AI tool so that they can follow your model, and this will help you anticipate what types of outputs students are likely to receive.

For the activities listed here, we used two of the more popular tools available at the time of this writing. Susan Edele's activity had students use ChatGPT, and Elizabeth Melick's activities had students use Claude. Whatever tool you choose, you should make sure that it has all the functionalities students will need to complete your activity. For example, in Melick's second activity, students will need an AI tool that allows users to upload documents for analysis.

2.1 Initial Interactions With AI (Edele)

In this section, Susan Edele offers an activity that helps students begin to interact with AI and learn what it is capable of doing. She includes steps for the activity and commentary on how students react to various steps in the activity and how to support them as they experiment with AI. This activity takes place over three class sessions for a course that meets three times a week.

Day 1: Discuss AI to determine what students already know

Step 1: Ask students if they know what artificial intelligence is

Commentary: When I posed the question, students looked away and no one responded. I asked again if they used auto-correct on their phones, or spellcheck or Grammarly or predictive text. I got a few nods, but no one raised a hand or said anything. I asked if anyone used ChatGPT or something similar. Again, no one said anything. Then, I raised my hand. I told the students I used ChatGPT as a tool for preparing lessons, creating sample essays, and summarizing data, like evaluations, to find themes and provide suggestions for improvement. It was not until I shared that I use is that students began to relax. A few students shared how they used AI – for research, for drafting, and for brainstorming.

Step 2: Briefly explain how ChatGPT works

- LLM creators "scrape" the internet for data so that the LLMs can "learn" from the creators of the texts, which is what is called "training" the AI tools.
- Explain that ChatGPT does have limitations and share the ways in which the LLM struggles (citations, arguments, false information, free account versus paid accounts).

Step 3: Small group brainstorm

- Break students into small groups to brainstorm how they could use AI/ChatGPT for writing (10–15 minutes).

- As students share their ideas, write the ideas on the board. (Be sure to take a photo of the board to reference in future class sessions.)

Day 2: Introduction to drafting with AI

Preparation

If possible, reserve a computer classroom or ask students to bring their laptops. Students can use their cell phones for this activity, but a computer is best.

Step 1: Practicing prompting

- Ask students to create a free account using ChatGPT or another AI tool. It can be helpful to have the entire class use the same tool so that everyone is looking at the same interface, but you might also allow students to use a different AI tool if they are already familiar with it.
- Briefly review the parts and the terms for AI LLM use (prompt, regenerate, sidebar of created documents, etc.).
- Ask the students to enter the following prompt: Write 500 words about ______________ (insert their favorite animal).

Commentary: As ChatGPT began writing, a few students were chattering in amazement. I walked the room to make sure everyone was doing OK with the instructions, and I heard students saying, “This is amazing!” and “Wow!!”

Step 2: Discussion of initial prompting

- Ask the students to share what animal they chose and record them on the board.
- Ask a few of the students who chose dogs as their animal to read the first few lines of their paragraphs. Then, ask the students who chose cats to read a few lines from their paragraphs.
- Next, ask students what they noticed about the language and word choice. There will likely be some similar words and phrases that were used in different paragraphs on the same

animals, though the paragraphs generated using the same or similar prompts will not be identical.

Step 3: Regenerate for specificity

- Ask the students to prompt the AI tool to regenerate the paragraph using a more specific breed or type of the animal they used for their first paragraph. For example, they might ask the AI tool to "Regenerate but make it a Dalmatian" or "Rewrite the paragraph but focus on a Siamese cat this time."
- Ask the students if the prompt response was appropriate – did ChatGPT answer the prompt?

Commentary: A few students said the prompt response was not what they wanted, so I encouraged them to regenerate with a more specific prompt. A few chatted with each other, bouncing ideas of each other and trying different wording in the prompts until they were satisfied with the results.

Step 4: Discuss results

- Ask a few students to read several lines from their paragraphs, and then ask students what they think of the paragraph.

Commentary: A few students stumbled over the vocabulary choices of Chat-GPT and said that the output was not their style or voice. I asked if they could revise the paragraph to make it in their style. A few said yes, and a few said no, they'd rather write the paragraph themselves, using the facts provided.

I asked them to use a prompt like this: In 500 words or fewer, tell me about the (insert specific animal). The students were pleased with the response, but still said they wanted to write the paragraph in their own voice. One student said his paragraph was definitely not his voice, but the assignment was complete, so he could "live with that."

Step 5: Using AI for outlining

- Ask the students to use the following prompt: Regenerate an outline for an 800-word essay on the (insert specific animal).

- After they have generated their outlines, ask students what they think of the outline – was it helpful? Did it meet the requirements for their last paper? If it did not, how could they revise the prompt to get better output?

Day 3: Reflect and share

Step 1: Small group discussion

- Ask students to get into small groups to discuss their ChatGPT experiences and make a list of pros and cons for using ChatGPT (10–15 minutes).
- Ask one person from each group to write their pros and cons on the board.

Step 2: Imagining uses for AI

- Refer back to the brainstorming list from Day 1 and ask students if they've thought of other ways to use ChatGPT now that they have experienced it. Add those ideas to the list.
- Ask students to write a short reflection (only to be read by the instructor) about their ChatGPT experiences. Did they like it? Will they use it? If so, how? If not, why? What do they still want to know/learn about AI or ChatGPT?

This activity offers students an accessible first interaction with an AI tool, which helps them to understand how to write and revise prompts. Through this activity, students also start to learn how to critically evaluate the text produced by the LLM and compare it to their own expectations for what they wanted the tool to produce and the expectations of the assignment.

2.2 Talking to Students About AI (Melick)

A core component of my incorporation of AI in my Composition classrooms is discussion of AI. Except for an occasional optional activity that uses AI, I do not include AI in any course assignments or activities without building in class time for pre- and post-activity discussions.

I discuss AI with my students during the first week of class, devoting 20–30 minutes of class time to presenting information about generative AI and discussing students' pre-existing thoughts about and attitudes toward AI. During this presentation and all subsequent discussions, I position myself as a curious skeptic regarding AI. I acknowledge that there are flaws in generative AI tools that have been met with valid criticism, but I also tell students that I don't believe we should be afraid of AI – instead, I suggest that it is good to gain some familiarity with the tools at the very least. Throughout the course, I encourage (and sometimes require) students to experiment with AI tools, but I also encourage them to consider AI output critically. My goal is to create a classroom space in which AI is a comfortable topic of discussion, but students also feel free to reject or embrace AI tools as part of their writing process.

To begin our first discussion of AI, I explain my position in relation to AI: I am part of a group of faculty on our campus who are interested in learning about AI and its capacities for enhancing education and workflows. I also briefly explain my policy for AI usage. Then, I ask students to join the conversation with two questions: "What do we know about AI tools? How do we feel about AI tools?" I also ask students who have experimented with AI to talk about how they have used it and how useful the tools were.

This conversation generally reveals a mix of feelings in the classroom. So far, my classes have included many students who have not used AI tools at all (or claim not to have), a few who have done a little bit of experimenting with it, and a few who have used it extensively. Attitudes vary in the same way that experience and familiarity vary: Some students are strongly opposed to the use of generative AI tools. (Anecdotally, these are often students who are majoring in creative or performing arts, and their objections are often rooted in IP and artistic concerns.) Some find the tools to be useful. Most students are inexperienced and have no firm opinions on the tools yet.

From there, I offer the class an overview of what generative AI is, how it works, and why generative AI has caused so much concern on a global scale, including issues of access, bias within the LLMs (and other AI tools), the potential for job losses, and the potential for the tools to hallucinate or produce false information (see Sections 1.1 and 1.2 for further discussion of these issues). I also talk about concerns specific to education and Composition classrooms and remind them that expectations for AI use will change based on the different contexts they find themselves in, pointing out that their other courses may not permit AI use, and their future employers may either encourage or prohibit the use of AI. We discuss potential benefits of using AI, as well as ways that AI could be incorporated into the writing process.

This conversation helps students to understand that AI is not "good" or "bad" and that it is OK to experiment with AI in my course. I make a point to continue this conversation throughout the course as we interact with AI several times. We continue to discuss how students might use AI and whether or not they want to continue using AI.

2.3 Writing With AI Activities (Melick)

For this section, I will include a narrative of two fictional students' experience in completing the first two AI-infused activities. These fictional students are designed to replicate experiences of actual students in my courses who have completed these activities in order to offer a sample of how students might complete these assignments. I include two fictional students in this section in order to offer representation for the varying viewpoints on AI expressed by students in my courses.

My first fictional student is named Elliot. He is majoring in fashion design and technology and hopes to someday work as a designer for an athletic clothing brand, which would allow him to draw on his love of sports and his passion for fashion design.

My second fictional student is Gwen, a business administration major with an emphasis in nonprofit administration. While Gwen is confident in her choice to major in business administration, she's not yet sure exactly what she hopes her eventual career path will look like.

For each of these students, I have included actual conversations with an AI tool that were generated as I posed as each student.

Activity 1: Topic Selection and Refinement

For this activity, students were prompted to use AI to choose or refine their topics for an argumentative research essay formulated as a "problem and solution" essay. As you'll see in the following prompts, the instructions for this activity offer suggestions for how students can collaborate with AI to choose and refine their topics, but the activity is also designed to encourage students to think critically about how to get the desired support from the AI tool and to experiment with formulating prompts.

Activity Instructions: Topic Selection and Refinement

Start here if you do not yet have an idea for a topic for your problem and solution essay.

- Tell the AI tool about the assignment and what you need (topic ideas). Think: what might be the best way to explain to the AI tool what the assignment is?
- Ask the AI tool for a *list of potential topics* rather than a single topic idea.
- You might tell the AI tool about some of your interests so that the tool can offer ideas that are tailored to you.

If you already have a topic, follow these steps:

- Tell the AI tool the broad topic you have selected for your writing project. Explain that you need help narrowing your focus and articulating your problem and solution. You should explain what the assignment is and the target length of the essay. Think: what might be the best way to explain to the AI tool what the assignment is?
- Ask the AI tool for a list of potential ways that you could narrow your focus for the essay.
- Ask the AI tool to suggest some ways you can explain the problem, along with several suggested solutions.
- From the AI tool's suggestions (or from your own thinking!) identify your narrowed topic as well as a potential solution you could discuss in your essay.

Sample Student Topic Activities

Sample 1: Elliot

Elliot:

Hi Claude. I have to write a 5–7 pg. paper for my English class. It's a problem and solution paper, so basically I have to talk about a problem and then also explain what the solution to the problem is. It's a research paper too, so I have to use 6 sources. 4 of my sources have to be scholarly. I'm trying to figure out what my topic will be for the paper. I'm a fashion design & tech major, so probably it should be something to do with that? But I also really love sports and so maybe I could write on something related to that. My professor said to pick something we care about. Can you give me 5 topic ideas?

AI (Claude) Response:

Sure, I can provide you with five topic ideas that relate to your interests in fashion design & tech and sports. Here they are:

1. The problem of fast fashion and its environmental impact: Discuss the issues surrounding fast fashion, such as pollution, waste, and unethical labor practices. Propose solutions like sustainable materials, circular economy principles, and consumer awareness.
2. The lack of diversity and inclusivity in the fashion industry: Address the problem of underrepresentation of various body types, ethnicities, and identities in fashion. Explore solutions such as diverse hiring practices, inclusive sizing, and showcasing a wider range of models.
3. The impact of technology on sports performance and injury prevention: Examine how advancements in technology, such as wearable devices and data analytics, can enhance athlete performance and reduce the risk of injuries. Discuss the implementation of these technologies and their potential drawbacks.
4. The issue of gender inequality in professional sports: Highlight the disparities in pay, media coverage, and opportunities between male and female athletes. Propose solutions like equal pay policies, increased sponsorship for women's sports, and challenging gender stereotypes.
5. The problem of counterfeit products in the fashion industry: Discuss the economic and social consequences of counterfeit fashion goods. Explore solutions such as blockchain technology for supply chain transparency, stronger intellectual property laws, and consumer education about the dangers of counterfeit products.

(*Continued*)

(Continued)

Sample 1: Elliot

Remember to choose a topic that genuinely interests you, as this will make the research and writing process more engaging. Once you've selected your topic, feel free to ask for further guidance on finding relevant sources or structuring your paper.

Elliot:

Ok those are pretty good ones. I think I probably want to talk about fast fashion. That's the one of those topics that I know the most about. Plus I'll probably be able to use this topic again for my major later on. I feel like it will be too much to talk about all of those topics for fast fashion in one paper. My professor said that we need to be careful to keep a narrow topic. What are some smaller topics within fast fashion I could use for this paper? I think it would be good to have something with a really clear solution because that's a big part of what the paper is about.

AI (Claude) Response:

Narrowing down your topic within the broader issue of fast fashion is a great idea to ensure a focused and manageable research paper. Here are some smaller topics within fast fashion that have clear solutions:

1. The environmental impact of textile waste in fast fashion: Discuss the problem of textile waste generated by fast fashion and its effects on the environment. Propose solutions such as implementing textile recycling programs, promoting upcycling and clothing repairs, and encouraging brands to adopt zero-waste design principles.
2. The use of hazardous chemicals in fast fashion production: Examine the issue of toxic chemicals used in clothing production and their impact on worker health and the environment. Explore solutions like implementing stricter regulations on chemical use, promoting the use of eco-friendly dyes and materials, and encouraging brands to adopt cleaner production methods.
3. The role of consumer behavior in perpetuating fast fashion: Examine how consumer demand for cheap, trendy clothing drives the fast fashion industry. Propose solutions such as promoting consumer education about the impacts of fast fashion, encouraging mindful consumption habits, and showcasing sustainable fashion alternatives.

These narrower topics within fast fashion provide specific problems and clear solutions that you can explore in-depth in your research paper.

(*Continued*)

(Continued)

Sample 1: Elliot

Elliot:

I think that consumer behavior one is what I'm probably going to go with. I know the most about that one because I've seen my friends and siblings get really into buying fast fashion stuff constantly over the past few years. And honestly, I'm kind of part of the problem too, so it might be good to learn about this. Can you give me a few more points to put in this paper or to think about for my topic?

AI (Claude) Response:

Absolutely! Here are some additional points and aspects to consider for your paper on the role of consumer behavior in perpetuating fast fashion:

1. The influence of social media and influencer culture: Discuss how social media platforms and influencers promote fast fashion consumption by constantly showcasing new trends and hauls, which can pressure consumers to keep up with the latest styles.
2. The psychology behind impulse buying: Explore the psychological factors that drive consumers to make impulse purchases in fast fashion, such as low prices, limited-time offers, and the fear of missing out (FOMO).
3. The environmental cost of overconsumption: Highlight the environmental consequences of excessive consumption in fast fashion, such as increased water usage, carbon emissions, and textile waste in landfills.
4. The impact of fast fashion on personal finances: Discuss how the constant pursuit of new, cheap clothes can lead to financial strain and debt for consumers, especially younger demographics.
5. The role of education in promoting sustainable consumption: Examine how education about the impacts of fast fashion and the benefits of sustainable alternatives can help shift consumer behavior towards more responsible purchasing decisions.
6. The potential of rental and secondhand fashion: Explore how promoting clothing rental services and secondhand markets can provide consumers with access to trendy fashion without the environmental and financial costs of constant new purchases.
7. The importance of individual action and collective change: Emphasize that while individual consumer choices are important, systemic change in the fashion industry also requires collective action, such as supporting sustainable brands, advocating for policy changes, and demanding transparency from fashion companies.

(*Continued*)

(Continued)

Sample 1: Elliot
As you develop your paper, consider including real-life examples, statistics, and personal anecdotes to illustrate the impact of consumer behavior on the fast fashion industry. Don't forget to explore counterarguments and potential challenges to implementing the proposed solutions, as this will demonstrate a well-rounded understanding of the topic.

Sample Student 2: Gwen

Gwen:

I need to write a paper for my English class. I'm having trouble choosing a topic. Here are the guidelines: Writing Project 3 is an argumentative research paper that focuses on proposing a solution to a problem or issue. The essay should have two sections: the first section should discuss a current problem, and the second section should propose a viable solution to the problem. The sections do not need to be equal in length, but each needs to be fully developed and supported by research.

The essay should include a discussion of a counterclaim or opposing viewpoint. This might be accomplished in the problem section, where an alternate understanding of the cause of the problem is explored. The opposing viewpoint might also be placed in the solution section, where an alternate solution could be discussed, or an argument as to why the solution may not be viable is addressed.

My major is business admin with nonprofit admin emphasis. I'm a freshman so I don't know that much about nonprofit yet. Can you give me some topics that go with my major?

AI (Claude) Response:

Certainly! Here are a few topic ideas related to your major in business administration with a nonprofit administration emphasis:

1. Problem: Inadequate funding for nonprofit organizations.
Solution: Propose innovative fundraising strategies or discuss the potential of social entrepreneurship.
2. Problem: Difficulty in measuring the impact of nonprofit programs.
Solution: Suggest the implementation of data-driven evaluation methods or the adoption of standardized metrics.

(Continued)

(Continued)

Sample Student 2: Gwen

3. Problem: High turnover rates among nonprofit employees.
Solution: Discuss strategies for improving employee retention, such as better compensation, professional development opportunities, or fostering a positive work culture.
4. Problem: Lack of diversity and inclusion in nonprofit leadership positions.
Solution: Propose initiatives to promote diversity, equity, and inclusion within nonprofit organizations, such as mentorship programs or unconscious bias training.
5. Problem: Ineffective collaboration among nonprofits with similar missions.
Solution: Suggest ways to foster partnerships, resource sharing, or mergers between nonprofits to increase their collective impact.
6. Problem: Challenges in attracting and retaining skilled volunteers.
Solution: Discuss strategies for volunteer recruitment, training, and recognition to ensure a stable and engaged volunteer base.
7. Problem: Difficulty in adapting to digital fundraising and engagement strategies.
Solution: Propose ways for nonprofits to leverage technology and social media to reach new donors and engage with their supporters more effectively.

These are just a few ideas to get you started. Remember to choose a topic that genuinely interests you and aligns with the course material you've covered so far. Once you've selected a topic, you can refine your problem and solution statements through research and further brainstorming.

Gwen:

The volunteer one sounds interesting to me. I'm actually doing the nonprofit emphasis because my cousin works at a nonprofit and I volunteer there sometimes. He said that they sometimes have trouble finding enough volunteers for their big projects. What would I talk about for a solution though?

AI (Claude) Response:

Great choice! Your personal experience volunteering at your cousin's nonprofit will add valuable insight to your paper. When discussing

(Continued)

(Continued)

Sample Student 2: Gwen

solutions for attracting and retaining skilled volunteers, consider the following points:

1. Targeted recruitment: Propose strategies for identifying and reaching out to potential volunteers with specific skills or backgrounds that align with the nonprofit's mission. This could include partnering with local universities, professional associations, or community groups.
2. Flexible volunteer opportunities: Suggest offering a range of volunteer roles with varying time commitments and responsibilities to accommodate different schedules and interests. This can include short-term projects, virtual volunteering, or skill-based opportunities.
3. Volunteer training and support: Emphasize the importance of providing comprehensive training and ongoing support to volunteers. This can include orientation sessions, mentorship programs, and regular check-ins to ensure volunteers feel prepared and valued.
4. Recognition and rewards: Discuss ways to acknowledge and appreciate volunteers' contributions, such as public recognition events, personalized thank-you notes, or small tokens of appreciation. Highlight how these gestures can boost morale and encourage long-term commitment.
5. Communicating impact: Propose regularly sharing stories and data that demonstrate the tangible impact of volunteers' efforts. When volunteers understand how their work contributes to the nonprofit's mission, they may feel more motivated to continue their involvement.
6. Fostering a sense of community: Suggest creating opportunities for volunteers to connect with each other and with the nonprofit's staff. This can include social events, team-building activities, or online forums where volunteers can share experiences and ideas.

In your paper, you can discuss how implementing a combination of these strategies can help nonprofits overcome the challenge of attracting and retaining skilled volunteers. Use your personal experiences and observations from volunteering at your cousin's nonprofit to support your arguments and provide real-world examples.

As a result of this activity, Elliot has chosen the topic of social media influence on fast fashion overconsumption and Gwen has chosen the topic of the difficulty that nonprofits experience in finding and retaining quality volunteers.

Activity 2: Article Analysis for Annotated Bibliography

This activity is a follow-up activity to the previous topic selection/refinement activity. These activities are usually completed in the same week. For this activity, I have students practice using an AI tool to analyze a scholarly article for the purpose of creating an annotation for the bibliography. This activity gives students practice in giving an AI tool very specific instructions and analyzing and critiquing its output.

Activity Instructions: Article Analysis Practice for Annotated Bibliography with AI

Find a potential source for your Annotated Bibliography for the problem and solution essay using our university library's databases. *Note: you will need a source that is a PDF or can be made into a PDF.*
Next, you will use an AI tool to analyze your article.

- Upload your article document to the AI tool.
- Use the AI tool to analyze the article and its suitability for this writing project.
  - Ask the AI tool for a summary of the article's argument and main points. It's often helpful to ask it to include page numbers for specific points, as this will help you verify the output and find useful passages.
  - Ask the AI tool to explain how the article might support the topic/argument of your essay, and whether or not it seems like a good choice for project. Is the article relevant to your topic? Will this article have useful statistics or examples to offer for your argument?
  - Ask the AI tool to evaluate the target audience for the article. Is this article written for other experts? Will a general reader (like you!) be able to follow the argument and understand the specialized language easily?

(*Continued*)

(Continued)

- Share the guidelines for Annotated Bibliography entries with the AI tool and ask it to create a sample entry for the article you have uploaded. You might consider sharing one of the sample annotation entries with the AI tool so that it knows what the entries should look like.
- Evaluate and revise the AB entry.
  - Compare the AB entry that The AI tool has created to the guidelines. Does it meet all of the requirements?
  - Check for accuracy. Are correct page numbers cited? Has the tool accurately summarized and evaluated the article?
- Make any adjustments that need to be made (either make corrections yourself or instruct the AI tool how to make those corrections).
- Post your annotation to the discussion board, and then start your reflection.

Activity Reflection

After completing the Annotated Bibliography activity, I ask students to reflect on their experience with the AI tool and share on a class discussion board. This is the first time that all students in the class use AI to create "polished" output rather than just as an idea generating tool, so it's important that they have a chance to reflect on their experience and evaluate how well the tool worked for them.

Instructions

Post your reflection questions to our discussion board in a separate post from your sample AB entry.

- How well did the AI tool you used (the AI tool or another tool) work for the tasks you were trying to accomplish using it?
- What did the AI tool do well? Do you think it did those tasks as well as you could have, or better than you could have done on your own?
- What did the AI tool struggle to do? When you encountered a task that the AI tool didn't do well, could you figure out how to instruct the tool to improve? What did you do if the AI tool couldn't "figure it out"?
- Do you think this AI tool would make you more efficient in research projects like WP 2 & 3? Why or why not?

(Continued)

(Continued)

- If you have not used an LLM AI tool like the AI tool before, how well did your experience with this activity match your expectations?
- As a result of your experience with the AI tool for this practice Annotated Bibliography activity, can you imagine using AI for other writing tasks? How likely are you to use the AI tool to help you complete your Annotated Bibliography?

Elliot uploads the first article he finds that seems relevant to the AI tool and asks the tool if the article seems relevant. The AI tool suggests that the article would be relevant and lists a few ideas from the article that might be useful for his essay. Then he shares the Annotated Bibliography entry guidelines with the AI tool and asks for a sample entry. The AI tool produces an entry that is three times longer than the assignment requires, and Elliot notices that it includes some quoted passages from the article but doesn't explain how that evidence could be used, as the guidelines require. Elliot asks the AI tool to regenerate the response, pointing out how the original attempt missed the mark. The second attempt meets all the requirements for the bibliography entry.

Gwen quickly finds an article she immediately knows will work for her essay, as it addresses how it is easier for nonprofits with bigger budgets to attract more volunteers. Knowing the article is relevant, she starts by having the AI tool generate an Annotated Bibliography entry. Gwen notices that the AI tool's output meets every standard for the assignment requirements, but she doesn't like the tone in the writing. She asks the AI tool to regenerate the entry and make the tone more appropriate for a college student. The AI tool's next attempt is too informal, using conversational phrases that Gwen knows aren't well-suited for academic writing and that she would never include in work for a course. She asks the AI tool to revise one more time, aiming for a level of formality somewhere in between the first and second attempts. The last attempt is a bit better than the first and the second attempts, but she realizes that the language in the entry still doesn't sound very much like her. She believes that she could continue to ask the AI tool to adjust its tone and word choice, but she decides to move on to using it to analyze a few other articles because she isn't as sure if the other articles she found will work well for her essay.

Sample Student Reflection Posts

After interacting with the AI tool, Elliot and Gwen complete the activity by posting their reflections on the discussion board. Here, Gwen and Elliot are reflecting on both their topic choice activity and the Annotated Bibliography activity

---

Elliot

The AI worked pretty well for what I wanted it to do. It was really good for choosing a topic and giving me ideas. That helped a lot because I found a topic I care about a lot, but I probably never would have thought of it by myself. It was really nice for me to have the help with coming up with ideas because that's something that can be hard for me sometimes. It did ok with annotated bibliography part too, even though its first try was way too long and didn't really hit every point it was supposed to. When I told it what it missed, it just rewrote it immediately and then that one was right.

After seeing what it did for the topic and the article review for the annotated bibliography, I do think it will help and it could make me more efficient. I found a bunch of articles today that might be kind of helpful, and so I think I might use the AI to help me choose which ones to actually use for me essay. It helped me figure out what the important parts in my article were too, so that will be helpful. The AI definitely exceeded my expectations by a mile. I haven't really used them before and I didn't realize they worked this well. I don't know if I will use it all the time, but I think I will definitely use this tool to help with big projects and analyzing sources.

Gwen

I was kind of surprised with how well the AI worked. It gave me good options for my topic and it did ok with the annotated bibliography part. My only issue with it is that is just does not sound like me at all. I am not a native English speaker and there were words that it put in there that I just would never use. I did try to get it

---

(*Continued*)

(Continued)

---

to write more like me, but I think it would take a lot of tries for it to get there. I guess that's not the end of the world, but it did bother me, and I don't know if I would feel comfortable with turning something in that sounded like a different person.

I guess the AI could help me be more efficient, but when I think about it, there is still a lot of work I will have to do with my sources for this essay. Even though this helped with the annotated bibliography, I still have to have all my evidence and sources for the actual essay. Between the words that I don't really know and feeling like I still don't know anything about the sources that I have to use in my essay, I'm feeling like I probably won't use AI for my essay. I think I will just be more comfortable with the project if I do this stuff myself. I can see myself using it for topic ideas in the future, though. That was actually really helpful, and it was a good starting place to get a bunch of topics I could choose and points I could write on.

Elliot liked using the AI tool and plans to use it to help him draft his essay, while Gwen acknowledges that it met expectations but intends not to use it for her writing project. These fictional responses reflect the sentiments of my actual students well: Many students were pleasantly surprised with the AI tools, but there were several students who expressed a determination not to use AI (even if they had a positive experience) because they preferred to write their work themselves. Some students also worried that relying on AI to analyze their sources wouldn't give them a strong enough understanding of their source material for their essays.

Whether students emerge from these activities enthusiastic to use AI as part of their writing or determined not to incorporate the tool in their writing process, the important result is that students have practiced prompting and evaluating AI output, comparing the generated text to assignment requirements to check if the output meets expectations. At the very least, these activities help students have an encounter with AI and practice in using AI to complete a task. The closing reflection helps students to think critically about how well the AI tool performed the requested task and carefully consider whether they will continue to use AI and what role it may play in their writing process.

Activity 3: Feedback on Rough Draft

After students have completed a rough draft of their problem and solution research essays, they have the option to use AI for feedback on their drafts as one potential reflection and revision activity.

Activity Instructions: Gathering Feedback from AI

For this activity, you will use an AI tool to gather feedback on your essay. You may want to gather feedback on high-order concerns, like the strength of your argument or the organization of your major ideas. You may also want help with low-order concerns, like editing for clarity or correcting sentence-level mistakes. Whether you are asking for help with high-order or low-order concerns, I encourage you to be open to the AI's suggestions but also to think critically about the suggestions the tool offers you. Just like the feedback you receive from your classmates during peer review, it's important to remember that you are the author of this essay, and you have the final choice on all elements of the piece of writing. Maintain your unique voice and perspectives even when incorporating feedback from peers or an AI tool.

Below, you'll find some suggestions for how an AI tool could be helpful in revising and improving your essay.

Using AI for High-Order Concerns

Step 1: Start by sharing the essay prompt or assignment guidelines so the AI tool understands the target learning outcomes and requirements for the essay. You may also want to add a brief overview of your topic, as well as any concepts regarding the assignment that were discussed in class. Think: what will the AI tool need to know about this assignment, this course, or you as the author in order to give you meaningful feedback?

Step 2: Next, copy and paste your full essay draft into the conversation. Ask specific questions about areas you'd like feedback on, such as:

- How well does this draft meet the stated learning outcomes/assignment goals? Are there any ways in which this draft does not meet the core requirements of this assignment?
- Have I offered a strong explanation for why this problem exists and why it needs to be solved? Does my proposed solution seem reasonable? Have I given a clear explanation of how the solution could be implemented?

(*Continued*)

(Continued)

- Are my arguments and reasoning clear and well-supported with evidence from my sources? Have I incorporated source material into my essay smoothly and effectively? Is there any information in this essay that seems like it needs a citation but doesn't have one?
- Does the organization and flow of ideas make sense? Are my paragraphs cohesive and focused on a single supporting point for my argument? Are there areas that need better transitions between ideas?

Step 3: Consider the feedback you have received from your peers and instructor on your draft. If there were any suggestions that you aren't sure how to incorporate, share those suggestions with the AI tool and ask for guidance on how to implement those suggestions successfully in your draft.

- Here is a sample prompt that asks for help with implementing a suggestion from a peer: "My classmate read my essay and said that I'm using my sources well in my paragraphs, but that the links between different paragraphs and sections in the essay aren't very clear. They said I need to add better transitions, especially between paragraphs 3 and 4 and 6 and 7. I've never really understood how to write transitions, so I don't know how to do this. Could you give me some examples of good transitions and some suggestions for how I could add transitions to those two spots in my essay?"

Using AI for Low-Order Concerns

You can request sentence-level feedback by asking the AI tool to suggest revisions for specific sentences or paragraphs that need improvement. Check your feedback from previous essays and note any sentence-level issue that your professor highlighted as an area for improvement and consider other sentence-level mistakes you know you tend to make.

Here are some sample prompts you might use to gather editing and proofreading suggestions from the AI tool:

- Are there any errors in punctuation, grammar, or spelling in this essay? If so, can you tell me which paragraphs they are in, and how I could correct them?
- Are there any areas that could use better word choice or phrasing?

(*Continued*)

(Continued)

- I sometimes struggle to use formal phrases and words. Are there any words or sentences in this essay that are too informal or conversational?
- My professor said that I need to try to use a mix of simple and complex sentences so that my writing isn't too choppy. Can you identify areas in my essay where I'm using a lot of short, choppy sentences so I can revise them?
- I accidentally write run-on sentences in my essays sometimes. Are there any run-on sentences in this essay?

Remember: AI tools can be very helpful for proofreading and revising support, but it's important to maintain your authentic and unique voice even when incorporating AI feedback (or feedback from classmates). Feel free to ignore phrasing suggestions from an AI tool that don't sound like your writing style, and remember that you can also guide the AI tool to offer suggestions that are a better match for your voice, vocabulary, and style.

2.4 Conclusion

The activities presented in this chapter offer a few ideas for how Composition instructors can begin to introduce their students to writing with AI and how they can frame these activities with thoughtful presentation and meaningful reflection in order to help students develop well-informed approaches to using AI tools. If you are an instructor who is just getting started with introducing AI to your Composition courses, we hope that these activity ideas have helped you imagine how AI could become part of your approach to teaching. We have offered just a few samples of how AI can be attached to specific writing projects, but there are many other ways AI can be introduced.

One approach that is not discussed here is the use of AI as a tool for simply learning about a topic. When teaching students how to prompt effectively with an AI tool, you might also have them learn about a topic relevant to the course. For example, you might have students use an AI tool to learn about professional communication conventions for emailing or writing resumés, cover letters, memos, and white papers. You might also have them use AI to learn about genre conventions within academic writing or how conventions differ among disciplines. You might also pair these activities with an in-class discussion or discussion board where students can share what they learned and evaluate the accuracy of AI output.

AI tools can also be used to help students consider the rhetorical situation for a writing project or adapt their arguments to suit different rhetorical situations. You might even use an AI-infused activity to help students learn about the rhetorical situation. For example, you might have students prompt an AI tool to generate an informative or argumentative message on a topic of their choosing. Then, students can prompt the AI tool to revise the statement multiple times, adapting voice and style to suit different audiences and contexts. A closing reflection can help students focus on the ways the AI tool adapted for different rhetorical situations, and this can even encourage students to critically examine how well the AI tool shifted its approach to suit different writing contexts. Identifying the strategies used for shifting genres and contexts in the AI tool's output can help students think about what aspects of their own writing they may need to adapt in order to communicate successfully in various contexts. (A similar assignment is included in the portfolio Daniel Plate describes in Chapter 3.)

Even if you are just getting started with teaching with AI, we hope you will consider the approach to teaching with AI offered in Chapter 3, which presents a way to teach Composition in which AI is fully infused in the writing process. Even if you are only ready to start incorporating a few AI activities into your classes, it is useful to consider what a more involved inclusion of AI would look like. As AI use increases, it is likely that many of us will increase our incorporation of AI in our Composition instruction, and Daniel Plate's discussion of how AI is used in his courses offers a useful model for what this can look like. Learning about what courses that involve more AI use look like can also help to inform your current efforts to introduce AI; knowing where your AI instruction might be headed can help you to make strategic choices about where to include AI in your courses now.

As you begin to incorporate AI in your Composition course, we hope you will remember that this is a field that is changing rapidly. Your first attempts at incorporating AI in your classes may not go smoothly, but this is the case for any effort to innovate and improve approaches to teaching. Bringing an open mind and willingness to experiment to your in-class AI activities will help your students to do the same, and modeling this mindset will likely offer a valuable learning experience to your students, helping them build skills with AI tools and positive approaches to new ways of learning and working at the same time.

3 AI Integration Through Portfolio Development

Daniel Plate

3.1 The Argument Portfolio and Writing "Up a Level" From Word-by-Word Composition

Let's assume for the sake of argument that students will use these AI tools. Let's accept their ubiquity. For whatever reason, universities have decided to allow students freedom in their use of AI tools for every stage of the writing process, everything from early brainstorming to paper drafts that are 90% generated by large language models (LLMs). Set aside for now whatever ethical or academic integrity questions that must be resolved in such a scenario. In this world of pervasive AI use, what course assignments and instructional techniques will serve the students best, and how should they be implemented? This chapter attempts an answer to these questions. In my case, the question is not hypothetical. I have allowed my Composition students to use LLMs in whatever way they choose in my courses, and I have evaluated the resulting papers as student work without requiring students to disclose whether and in what ways they have used LLMs in their submissions.

I started experimenting with this way of teaching Composition in Fall 2022 prior to the release of ChatGPT near the end of that semester. During that semester, my students completed an experimental assignment in which they researched the AI writing assistants available as free tools, attempted to write portions of essays with those tools, and reported on the results. Some of my stronger students that semester discovered an interesting website created by a company named OpenAI and argued for the superiority of a model available through that site named

DOI: 10.4324/9781003507949-4

GPT-3. The general conclusion of almost all the students in that course in Fall 2023 was that the tools were not capable of college-level writing, though many of the students expressed satisfaction with the opportunity to experiment.

Then ChatGPT was released. Over the winter break, I expanded my plans for providing pedagogical support for students choosing to write with AI, and in my Spring 2024 courses, I rolled out a portfolio project for a maximalist approach to integrating AI into the writing classroom. The results have been varied. This chapter will not provide quantitative data on AI use; instead, I will describe the argument portfolio assignment I settled on for my AI-maximalist course and give a clear-eyed assessment of the benefits of such a course and the challenges involved in teaching it effectively.

This chapter is underpinned by research I have done quite recently into advanced applications of AI in enhancing the educational experience beyond the initial, formative, or evaluative stages of student writing (Hutson et al., 2022; Hutson & Plate, 2023a; 2023b; 2023c; 2024; Hutson et al., 2024; Plate & Hutson, 2022; 2024). All of these articles present results from involving AI tools or machine learning and NLP techniques in English courses, mostly in Composition but also in creative writing teaching. During my experiments with coding as a support for pedagogy, I have been insistent that AI should not be used only for preliminary tasks such as topic selection or draft feedback; the student should be given experience with a comprehensive integration of AI throughout the entire writing process.

The idea of the argument portfolio assignment is quite simple. It has three sections. The first is a series of short pieces with different rhetorical contexts, audiences, and styles. These are AI-generated pieces that allow the student to experiment with world-building around an argumentative thesis. The second part of the portfolio is a formal argument paper following academic conventions for a well-researched, thesis-driven argument. The third is a reflective essay commenting on the portfolio creation process. What I am calling the "world-building pieces" take advantage of three strengths of the new AI tools: high-volume text generation, creative idea generation, and highly developed rhetorical skill. LLMs really have enabled an entirely new kind of writing. Students are empowered to create as many written pieces as they choose to over a short period with focused effort. The varied styles and audiences of these pieces give students a kind of creative laboratory for testing out an argumentative thesis for many different audiences and imagined contexts. This experiment can result in a formal paper drawing on a new kind of argument iteration.

This is the argument portfolio assignment description I give my students at the beginning of the course.

Final Portfolio: Exploring an Argument Through AI-Assisted Writing

The argument portfolio is the central writing project of the course, accounting for 30% of the overall grade. This portfolio is designed to showcase your ability to develop a coherent and persuasive argument across multiple genres and for various audiences. The primary emphasis is on exploring the implications of your argument and adapting it strategically to different rhetorical situations. The portfolio must include the following 20 pieces:

1. Formal academic argument paper with research sources
2. 18 AI-assisted rhetorical variations related to the argument paper
3. A 2–3 page reflective essay on your experience with AI-assisted writing and portfolio construction

On the AI-Assisted Rhetorical Variations

The 18 AI-assisted pieces are essential to the portfolio, as they provide an opportunity to probe the ramifications of your central argument by engaging with different audiences using a variety of genres. These variations should demonstrate your ability to adapt your core argument effectively to diverse rhetorical situations.

Using AI tools like ChatGPT, you will be able to generate a much higher volume of writing than would otherwise be feasible, enabling you to experiment with arguing for your position in multiple contexts. During class and in our course materials, you will be givenmany examples of AI-generated pieces related to arguments we have discussed in class. These are real-world kinds of writing that show how our arguments fit into contexts outside the classroom.

(Continued)

(Continued)

Potential genres for the AI-assisted pieces include:

- Blog posts
- News articles
- Editorials
- Academic papers
- Speeches
- Infographics
- Open letters
- Policy briefs
- Social media posts

It does not take long to see the distance between the use of AI encouraged by the assignment and the more standard criteria for AI use that have shown up in official documents such as university AI policies and institutional citation guidelines. An article from February of 2024 in the APA Style section of the American Psychological Association site voices a very common policy recommendation with respect to the use of AI: "In this post, I discuss situations where students and researchers use ChatGPT to create text and to facilitate their research, not to write the full text of their paper or manuscript" (McAdoo, para. 2). This is the distinction most frequently made in discussions of AI and academic writing. AI tools should be used for brainstorming, planning, and perhaps outlining, but the word-by-word text of a document should be purely human work.

The argument portfolio my students write for me is based on a different principle: Students can benefit from having an AI tool take care of generating the word-by-word language of a student-curated collection of documents and moving their critical thinking process "one level up" from the individual words to the rhetorical structure of those documents. To see how students work with LLMs in my course to fulfill the assignment requirements, I will recreate in this chapter the work of an imagined student named Jamie. The AI prompts and assignments described here as written by the student were written by me (using Claude and ChatGPT), but they accurately represent the work of many students in my Composition courses during these first 15 months of teaching with AI in the classroom.

That last sentence needs a little more explanation. Each of the sample student assignments provided in this chapter were generated using either ChatGPT or one of the Claude models using prompts I modeled after prompts I gave to my students as examples. These portfolio pieces are representative of the kinds of pieces students generated for their argument portfolios, but in order to present a cohesive portfolio idea, I invent a student named Jamie, provide this student with a long-abiding fascination with a "non-academic" topic (telepathy), and show how this student uses ChatGPT (and other AI tools) to explore many different contexts for thinking about that topic, eventually producing a number of documents for a variety of audiences and seeing how this topic can be transformed into a completely different kind of formal argument. All of this would still be possible if the student were to write every word of every document; but in a course that usually requires 3–4 papers with rough and final drafts of each, asking the students to write an additional 15–20 documents presenting the core idea in many different rhetorical forms and imagined contexts is not in line with plausible expectations for freshmen writers.

Though the AI tools that make this portfolio-generating process possible are new, two pedagogical principles motivating the work are very old. The first is the philosophical thought experiment. What I describe for my students using the popular term "world-building" could also be called "extended thought experiments" with some additional writer-audience scaffolding. The thought experiment has a venerable pedigree I explain further on in the chapter. Many students enjoy these "what-if" questions and the range of topics that emerge from them. The second pedagogical idea could be traced back to the Renaissance scholar and writer Erasmus and his use of the rhetorical technique of *copia* in his instruction of writing pupils. The simple fact is that LLMs are astonishingly productive. The volume of text one can generate is almost theoretically infinite. They are also a portal to as much world-building creativity as one chooses to pursue. Binding high-volume writing and rhetorical creativity together is the concept Erasmus termed *copia*. Opening his work *Copia: Foundations of the Abundant Style*, one finds a method for instruction in writing, rhetorical variation, that has intriguing potential for this LLM moment. How many different ways can one say, "Your letter delighted me greatly" (Erasmus's base example for copious variation)? How many different ways can a student make an argument with an LLM?

Through generating texts in a wide range of genres, styles, and formats, LLMs give students as much practice as time permits in drafting arguments and adapting them to different audiences, contexts, and writing purposes. This rhetorical diversity shows the student what it means to develop a repertoire for communicating effectively in a world defined by many technological forms and venues for messaging, where the ability to tailor one's text to different rhetorical situations is increasingly important (Darics, 2015). Students can build experience with varying a single theoretical argument for different audiences and learn to read a context and purposely shape a persuasive approach for that context. The most successful writers are those who can adapt their strategies and techniques to meet the needs of each unique rhetorical situation (Vieregge, 2020). Experimenting with different genres, styles, and formats through AI-assisted writing involves students in making rhetorical choices that situate their argument in at least some of the possible worlds the students might someday encounter.

3.2 Two Examples of Argument Portfolio Pieces

To see how the idea of the portfolio might work for a particular student, consider the case of a student I have named Jamie and two of the portfolio pieces Jamie generates using the Claude 2.0 LLM-based chatbot. Jamie is developing a kind of neologism, a concept he terms "cognitive privacy" or "cognitive liberty," themes inspired by Jamie's interest in telepathy and telepathic characters within popular culture. In Section 3.3, I will describe in more detail the actual AI-generated documents Jamie uses to move from a childhood interest in telepathy as a fascinating theme in science fiction to the concepts he chooses as possible topics for his portfolio and formal argument paper. The direct mind-to-mind communication of telepathy stories turns into an investigation into broader societal issues such as employer surveillance and personal privacy, eventually drawing parallels to philosophical discussions on freedom and autonomy similar to those articulated by John Stuart Mill (1859) in excerpts handed out for the students in Jamie's class to read. Jamie's portfolio project begins with a personal preference for a TV sub-genre that evolves into the academic research process part-way into the course, research directed toward the general idea of different forms of human communication and more gradually into technological advancements in communication. Jamie uses class readings that obliquely connect with his interests in telepathy and then cognitive liberty to survey as much research as possible in the scope of the course, philosophical debates about freedom of speech and bodily autonomy.

As he moves into the pieces for the argument portfolio itself, Jamie uses AI prompting to create several smaller rhetorical variations based on a rough draft of an argument paper about cognitive freedom and privacy. These variations push Jamie to experiment with different styles and audiences, ranging from academic essays to opinion pieces, each iteration helping him refine his arguments and deepen his understanding of the subject. This iterative process, supported by AI-generated content, exemplifies the potential of AI to enhance student engagement with complex topics and bring about a more dynamic and reflective writing process.

One example of Jamie using a targeted AI prompt to create a non-academic piece of writing shows how Jamie's idea for a topic at the beginning of the course (telepathy) can be encouraged in a pretty low stakes way. Jamie can generate something about telepathy, see some of the ideas latent in that topic, and start a kind of meta-brainstorming process that will eventually lead to the more argument-focused concepts of bodily autonomy, cognitive privacy, and workplace communications that will eventually figure in his academic argument paper. This is the first portfolio piece written by Jamie in the course. The prompt has three stages. In the first stage, Jamie asks the AI to help him imagine a TV show with a telepathy theme. This showcases a novel kind of freedom enabled by LLMs. If a student doesn't find an existing TV show to analyze, the student can ask the LLM to make one up and shape the thought experiment of the project from the ground up.

The second stage of the prompting is second-order world-building. The student asks the LLM to create a Wikipedia-style page describing the imagined TV show and giving a more focused description of one episode from the show that brings out the theme the student is interested in at the beginning of the class. This prompting practice is very important. Students need experience prompting the LLMs and seeing what they are capable of generating. This also gives them a first-hand taste of one of the most serious downsides of LLMs for academic writing, the fact that they can create pages of "facts" that seem to describe reality but actually bring to life entirely made-up scenarios. The final stage of the prompting activities is world-building at one more remove as the student finally generates a document that will end up in the portfolio itself. In this case, the student writes a blog post about the made-up episode from the LLM-imagined TV show.

Jamie

Help me create a made-up sci-fi TV series; I am trying to develop a scene from an episode of a made-up TV series that has a moment of telepathy in it. Write a Wikipedia-style description of the TV series and the episode with the telepathy in it. My first portfolio piece will be about this made-up show.

AI (Claude) Response:

[Claude creates a Wikipedia-style write-up of a show it titles *MindLink* that includes scenarios related to telepathy.]

Jamie:

Now help me write a blog post about the episode. The blog post should be critical about something that makes me pretty anxious

---

(*Continued*)

(Continued)

whenever I watch shows about telepathy. I feel like my personal space or freedom would be getting stepped on if I were one of the characters in the show and trying to keep my thoughts separate from the thoughts of other characters in the show.
Make sure to use some really specific made-up details from the show/episode in the blog post.

AI (Claude) Response:

"*MindLink*'s 'Silent Whispers': A Troubling Depiction of Telepathic Privacy Invasion"
As a long-time fan of the science fiction series *MindLink*, I've always been captivated by its exploration of telepathic abilities and their impact on society. However, after watching the recent episode "Silent Whispers," I find myself increasingly uneasy about the show's portrayal of telepathic communication and its implications for cognitive liberty.
In the episode, Sarah, one of the Linked characters, engages in a silent telepathic conversation with Agent Thompson, a government official who is secretly Linked himself. While the scene is undeniably tense and well-acted, it raises some troubling questions about the nature of telepathic privacy and consent.

Throughout the exchange, both Sarah and Thompson attempt to probe each other's minds for information, while simultaneously shielding their own thoughts. This mental tug-of-war may make for compelling television, but it also normalizes the idea that telepathic individuals have the right to invade others' minds without their explicit consent.

As someone who has long been fascinated by the concept of telepathy, I've always been drawn to the idea of the enhanced connection and understanding it could bring. However, episodes like "Silent Whispers" force me to confront the darker side of this ability. If telepathic communication becomes a reality, how can we ensure that our innermost thoughts and feelings remain our own? How do we protect our cognitive liberty in a world where others may have the power to access our minds at will?

The episode also hints at a larger conspiracy involving the government's exploitation of Linked individuals, which only compounds my concerns. If those in power have the ability to read and manipulate the minds of others, the potential for abuse and control is staggering. This storyline serves as a chilling reminder of the importance of safeguarding our mental privacy and autonomy, especially in the face of emerging technologies.

(*Continued*)

(Continued)

While *MindLink* is a fictional series, it has always excelled at exploring real-world issues through the lens of science fiction. “Silent Whispers” is no exception, as it forces us to grapple with the complex implications of telepathic abilities and their potential impact on our fundamental rights and freedoms.

As the series continues, I hope that it will delve deeper into these important questions and offer a more nuanced exploration of telepathic ethics and privacy. In the meantime, “Silent Whispers” serves as a thought-provoking reminder of the need to protect our cognitive liberty, both in the world of *MindLink* and in our own rapidly evolving technological landscape.

Notice in the prompt Jamie creates for the blog post about the made-up show an interesting development in his thinking. Jamie wants the LLM to help him write something that is “critical about something that makes me pretty anxious.” Jamie knows, at the beginning of the course, that he enjoys telepathy (a kind of technology) but that he also feels anxiety about some possible consequences of telepathy. This tension has potential for a possible argument topic. This part of the prompt moves Jamie from simply enjoying the idea of telepathy in pop culture to a possible argumentative stance. It’s important to see here that Jamie does not need to write the word-by-word argument of this particular blog post in order to benefit from the metacognitive shift in his portfolio. He can feel the shift toward a new idea he will eventually call “cognitive liberty,” and he can do this relatively quickly through the prompting process. Jamie’s fascination with telepathy has gotten more complicated now that he worries about how telepathy creates transparency in ways that make him anxious as to their implications, and this discomfort is part of the portfolio-long revision process.

This highlights a fact about LLMs that makes many people quite uncomfortable. LLMs are not only capable of generating an unprecedented volume of writing. These models also augment student creativity in very unexpected ways. Using the vast knowledge base and generative capabilities of LLMs, students can explore their topics from unconventional angles, discover surprising connections, and spark their own creative thinking. Unlike traditional writing tools, which are largely passive and reactive, LLMs are dynamic, generative, and frequently unpredictable. Drawing on their vast training data, these models can make surprising connections between seemingly disparate concepts, texts, and contexts, opening up new avenues for exploration and analysis (Besta et al., 2024). When students engage with an LLM, they are not simply receiving feedback or suggestions; they are entering into a collaborative creative process in which the AI might become a genuine source of inspiration and discovery. Through responding to the outputs of a model with their own ideas, interpretations, and revisions, students become active participants in a reciprocal creative exchange that can lead to insight and breakthrough (Wale & Bogale, 2021). For example, an LLM might generate a prompt that combines the topic of a student with an unexpected metaphor, a historical event, or a philosophical concept, inviting the student to consider their argument from a fresh perspective. The engagement with these novel combinations allows students the ability to break free from habitual ways of thinking and develop a more flexible, inventive approach to their writing. This approach has similarities with the creative writing prompt or writing exercise I will explore a bit further in the conclusion of this chapter (Kiteley, 2005).

It will also pay off to expand the definition of what counts as "creative" in a writing course. Creativity in writing is often approached through the lens of style or loosening restrictions on self-expression. LLMs do permit this kind of creativity, and instructors can decide whether to encourage that kind of use. In my work with the argument portfolio, I have taught students to "move up a level" and take advantage of the ability of LLMs to create contexts around the formal academic argument essay. Students can imagine scenarios in which a person might write a memo or plan an event with perhaps only oblique relevance to the paper, but because these written pieces can be generated quickly by the LLM, the student can sketch out possible written contexts for their argument without the pressure young writers often feel to use everything they write. This move away from a focus on word-by-word creativity and toward larger context world-building for the formal paper does appeal to many students.

A second example of this is the decision of our imagined student to think through the different sides of the debate over transparency and disclosure of AI tools in academic, corporate, or professional writing. Jamie started from ideas about telepathy, moved from there to questions about workplace (and classroom) surveillance and eventually to the pressing controversy over whether the use of AI in writing ought to be disclosed to readers, a corporate boss, or an instructor in a course. One way to investigate the debate is to read news and articles about it, and Jamie does this, but he also uses the creative potential of LLMs to imagine the topic from a different angle.

Jamie:

I want you to help me write a product review for a tech blog, evaluating a new AI-powered writing assistant and discussing the importance of transparency in its development and use. This blog is imaginary, and the AI writing tool is also made-up.

Make up all the details of the writing assistant – name, specs, some news about its use. Balance the product review as a practical thing and something I can use to make a strong argument. I want to express the worries I have about writers, workers, and students being required to state upfront when they use AI for their writing. Include my opinion about NOT requiring transparency or disclosure in the use of these tools. Any user of AI should be free to use them *without disclosing the working methods they have employed.*

AI (Claude) Response:

Product Review: WordWeavr AI – A Powerful Writing Assistant with a Transparency Problem

As an avid follower of the latest developments in AI-powered writing tools, I was thrilled to get my hands on WordWeavr AI, the new kid on the block that's been making waves in the tech world. Developed by Silicon Valley startup CogniTech, WordWeavr promises to revolutionize the way we write by offering advanced features like contextual analysis, tone adaptation, and even creative story generation.

(*Continued*)

(Continued)

First, let's talk about the good stuff. WordWeavr's user interface is sleek, intuitive, and highly customizable. The app seamlessly integrates with all major word processors and even offers a standalone web version for those who prefer to work in the cloud. The real magic, however, lies in its AI-powered writing assistance.

As someone who writes across multiple genres and styles, I was impressed by WordWeavr's ability to adapt to my voice and provide tailored suggestions for everything from word choice to sentence structure. The app's contextual analysis is truly next-level – it not only understands the content of your writing but also picks up on subtle cues about your intended audience and purpose.

One of the most exciting features of WordWeavr is its "Creative Spark" mode, which uses advanced language models to generate entire paragraphs or even short stories based on your input. While the results can be hit-or-miss, I found this tool to be an incredible source of inspiration and a great way to break through writer's block.

But here's where things get a bit thorny. In recent weeks, there have been growing calls for greater transparency around the use of AI writing tools, with some even advocating for mandatory disclosure whenever these apps are used. As an ardent believer in cognitive liberty and the right to privacy in one's creative process, I find these demands deeply troubling.

The beauty of tools like WordWeavr is that they empower users to express themselves more effectively and efficiently, regardless of their background or skill level. But this empowerment comes with an implicit trust – a trust that the user's autonomy and agency will be respected, and that they will not be forced to disclose the intimate details of their writing process.

Imagine if we demanded that every writer disclose whether they used a thesaurus, a grammar checker, or even a human editor. Such a requirement would be rightly seen as an infringement on creative freedom and an unnecessary burden on the writer. The same principle should apply to AI-powered tools like WordWeavr.

Moreover, the insistence on transparency and disclosure ignores the reality that writing is an inherently personal and multifaceted process. The line between human and machine input is often blurry, and attempting to untangle it for the sake of some misguided notion of "purity" or "authenticity" is a futile and ultimately harmful endeavor.

CogniTech, to its credit, has been upfront about its commitment to user privacy and has explicitly stated that it will not bow to pressure to build in any sort of "disclosure" feature into WordWeavr.

(*Continued*)

(Continued)

In an age where our creative choices are increasingly being policed and scrutinized, this commitment to user autonomy is laudable and necessary.

So, where does that leave us? As a writing tool, WordWeavr is undeniably powerful and full of potential. Its AI-powered features are a genuine breakthrough and a boon for writers of all stripes. But as a symbol of the larger debate around transparency and disclosure in the use of AI, it also represents a critical flashpoint.

My verdict? WordWeavr is a stellar product that deserves a place in every writer's toolkit. But more importantly, it's a reminder that our creative autonomy and right to privacy must be fiercely defended, even – and perhaps especially – in the face of technological change. The future of writing is AI-powered, but it must also be free.

4.5/5 stars

The review of WordWeavr, the made-up AI writing tool, is a kind of warm-up exercise for some aspects of Jamie's argument paper. The style is informal, but the ideas are important, and the fact that Jamie can generate the review (and the product itself!) very quickly with the LLM is just one more tool available to a student writer attempting to understand how his argument might play out in a real-world context. By situating his discussion of cognitive liberty within the context of a made-up product and review for that same product, Jamie creates a self-contained world in which his ideas can be explored and tested. The act of creative world-building requires a significant degree of imagination, logical consistency, and rhetorical skill. It is not always clear where creativity exists. Does creativity only exist in the word-by-word generation of words in the mind that the writer then transfers to the page? Or can creative work also happen at the level of editing, selecting, and curating existing content (generated, in this case, by the LLM)? And in this case, perhaps the student exercises a high degree of creativity by taking a plausible scenario that emerged during the prompting process and then reshaping and rethinking that scenario as material out of which to advance a persuasive argument.

This kind of argument-building is not entirely novel. There is a long tradition within philosophy, for example, of constructing thought experiments to test ideas. From John Searle's Chinese Room argument (Searle, 1980) to Robert Nozick's (1974) Experience Machine or, going back further, even Descartes's creation of the Evil Genius character controlling his sensations of the physical world, creative, and imaginative play has had an important role to play in the construction of rigorous arguments. In the context of this imagined student portfolio, a particular thought experiment also plays a role. Judith Jarvis Thomson's Famous Violinist thought experiment exploring the implications of various positions on abortion plays a role in Jamie's thinking about telepathy, AI, and cognitive autonomy (Thomson, 1971). AI tools are ideally suited for explorations of this kind, both because of their deep knowledge of the history of philosophical thought experiments and their ability to brainstorm with students about novel thought experiments (Mitchell, 2021).

The success of this creative endeavor is evident in the way that Jamie's letter balances the speculative and the real, and the imaginative and the analytical. Even as he engages with the fictional premise of telepathic technology, Jamie remains grounded in the real-world stakes of his argument, drawing connections to urgent contemporary issues such as data privacy, mental health, and the ethical implications of emerging technologies. The ability to use creative speculation as a tool for rigorous intellectual inquiry is a hallmark of effective AI-assisted writing, and it demonstrates the powerful role that LLMs can play in fostering unexpected connections and insights.

The creative potential of AI-assisted writing is not limited to the generation of fictional scenarios or speculative arguments. LLMs can also help students do creative work in more subtle, iterative ways by encouraging them to approach their ideas from multiple angles, experiment with different styles and voices, and revise their work in response to unexpected prompts and suggestions (Sharples, 2022). To support this iterative creativity, you should encourage your students to engage with the AI in a spirit of open-ended exploration and play. Rather than simply using the LLM to generate a single, fixed output, students can be encouraged to engage in a back-and-forth dialogue with the model, responding to its suggestions with their own ideas, questions, and revisions. This dialogic approach to AI-assisted writing can help students break out of fixed patterns of thinking and writing and discover new possibilities for expression and argumentation.

One way to facilitate this iterative creative process is through the use of open-ended prompts that encourage students to explore their topics from multiple perspectives. For example, students might be asked to generate a series of rhetorical variations that approach their arguments from the point of view of different stakeholders, historical figures, or even inanimate objects (Dong & Lu, 2020). When students are forced to consider their ideas from unconventional angles, these prompts can help disrupt habitual ways of thinking and writing and open up new avenues for creative exploration. Another strategy for fostering iterative creativity is to encourage your students to experiment with different styles, genres, and forms of expression. In my experience with the AI-augmented portfolios so far, it is better to push students away from "obvious" creative output like short fiction, poetry, and songs and more toward the existing genres of work and professional life. Students don't immediately think of this as creativity, but it certainly is, and engaging the imagination in anticipating the worlds within which their topics could exist helps them think about their writing and their lives. LLMs are capable of generating a wide range of textual outputs, from formal academic prose to casual social media posts, and everything in between (Meier, 2024). The ability to move between different registers and forms of expression is not only a valuable creative skill but also an essential competency for success in a rapidly changing communication landscape.

3.3 AI Tools as Support for the Revision Process

It is very difficult to persuade students to make large-scale revisions to their work. By the time they complete a full draft of a paper, most students feel they have moved beyond the stage of deleting full paragraphs or sections of the paper in favor of a new argument or the use of a different source. Everyone teaching in Composition is familiar with the equation many students make of "revision" with "proofreading."

As seen in the description of Jamie's development of his portfolio using AI tools, the use of an LLM for generating many different versions of an argument allows a student to make very significant revisions to a "draft" of the paper without being aware that this is what they are doing. The student is simply trying on different versions of an argument by seeing how it looks in different settings. This, again, is too much to ask if the student must write every word of every document in the course.

Peter Elbow's (1973) conceptualization of writing as a "mysterious" and "fuzzy" process provides valuable context for understanding why students often struggle with substantive revision and how AI tools might help address this challenge (pp. 12–13). Elbow argues against the "commonsense method" of trying to "figure out your meaning" before writing, asserting that meaning is actually "not what you start out with but what you end up with" (p. 15). He emphasizes that "writing is a way to end up thinking something you couldn't have started out thinking" (p. 15).

This perspective helps us think about why students resist major revisions. They put significant effort into crafting a complete draft, so they feel committed to the ideas and arguments they've already made. Asking them to discard or significantly rework substantial portions feels like a waste of effort, throwing away the language they worked so hard to build. However, Elbow's (1973) model suggests that this early draft should be seen as an exploratory step in an ongoing process of discovery. Elbow's approach aligns well with the potential of AI tools to encourage students toward deeper revision. By quickly generating multiple variations on a concept or argument, the AI can help students see their initial drafts as provisional, rather than fixed. Iterating through machine-generated alternatives may reduce the personal investment that leads students to cling to their original versions. Elbow emphasizes the need to "encourage conflicts or contradictions" as "the most fruitful situation to be in" (p. 50), even though it often feels frustrating. AI tools can promote this productive discomfort by confronting students with many quickly iterated possibilities and compelling them to critically evaluate and evolve their thinking. Used thoughtfully, AI offers a means of realizing Elbow's vision of writing as a way to "grow and cook" meaning through a dynamic, recursive process (p. 15).

A requirement of the portfolio is that students must not repeat rhetorical forms. If the student writes a blog post about a TV show for one piece, the student cannot continue to write blog posts for other portfolio submissions. This pushes the students to imagine a narrative involving their argument as it moves from one context of writing, thinking, and debating the topic to other discourse worlds. It is especially valuable to give students experience with genres of writing that are different from either typical creative writing pieces (fiction, poetry, creative non-fiction) or standard academic assignments (compare/contrast, narrative, formal argument, etc.). LLMs themselves are able to recommend rhetorical variations that come from professional workplace writing and organizational writing, which gives students a window into worlds they might choose to inhabit. A brief explanation of the pieces in Jamie's portfolio demonstrates the variety of tone and language as well as the development of several possible thesis claims for a more formal argument paper.

Here is a running list of items in Jamie's portfolio with annotations.

- Blog post about a TV show with themes of telepathy
- Letter to university newspaper arguing that telepathy-enabling technologies would invade privacy
- Student comments in online forum; follow-up to letter to university newspaper in which Jamie acknowledges the need for community but expresses worries about how employers might use telepathy-like technologies to surveil employees and their work

- Informal essay in online sci-fi magazine about themes of telepathy in the *Patternist* novels of Octavia Butler
- A letter to Jamie's representative in the U.S. Congress pushing support for brain-to-brain communication technologies as well as ethical guidelines for these technologies that advocate for individual privacy

This last letter is quite interesting in that it demonstrates the kind of "fork-in-the-road" moments students will have while building extended assignments such as an argument portfolio with AI tools. Up to this point, Jamie has been very concerned about certain dystopian visions of telepathy he has picked up over the years from TV shows, movies, and novels. The first four pieces in his portfolio push back against any "real-life" technologies that have started to show telepathy-like capabilities because he worries about living in a world in which these technologies are not created with strong ethical guidelines in place. However, in the letter to his representative, the AI generates two different kinds of concern about such technology:

> However, as with any powerful technology, the development of BCIs also raises important ethical and societal questions. How do we ensure that these devices are used responsibly and equitably? How do we protect the privacy and autonomy of individuals in a world where our very thoughts may be accessible to others? These are complex challenges that will require careful consideration and robust public dialogue.

The first is a generic ethical concern expressed using typical AI language. Nothing specific, no particular ethical violation, is described in the first two sentences. The third sentence, however, gives Jamie a nudge that eventually becomes the focus of his entire portfolio and the formal academic argument paper itself. The use of "privacy" and "autonomy" here shift the focus from a general, more collective understanding of the ethical to an individual one that will prioritize individual liberty as the central point.

- A memo-style email to Jamie's employer protesting his employer's purchase of a much more powerful work surveillance technology.

This document also shifts Jamie's topic focus. There are many reasons a person might give for objecting to one's employer having access to the moment-to-moment work patterns of an employee. These protests might be categorized under the umbrella of "privacy" but still differ. In theory, Jamie could object to this invasion of employee privacy as an economic struggle between the employer and employee in which the employee is struggling against the employer's ownership of the energy and time of the employee. The language of the memo itself gives Jamie another option: "the use of such invasive technology would be a serious infringement on our fundamental right to cognitive liberty."

Up until this memo, Jamie was not thinking about the question of whether an employee should be able to make decisions about *how the work gets done*. This is less an economic ownership question and more a question of what computer scientists call a "black box." In software development, a black box is some component in code that will accomplish a well-defined task without revealing the means by which that task is accomplished. This is a very important principle in software decision that maintains a clear separation of concerns between one part of the code and another. The language of the memo, generated by the AI, has introduced a possible new direction for research, and Jamie decides to take it.

This does not show Jamie's word-by-word thinking being "replaced" by a machine. At issue here is something quite different. At what level does the human contribution to the topic development process take place as Jamie uses the AI to generate the portfolio pieces? Jamie is not contributing the individual words to the portfolio pieces. He is noticing the branching possibilities in his topic as word-by-word contributions are made by the AI, and he chooses to pick up on some of these possibilities and let others drop.

- An email to Jamie's philosophy professor for another class. In this email, Jamie is objecting to his professor's decision to steer Jamie away from a philosophy paper about the twin principles of bodily autonomy (such as in the abortion or drug-use debates) and cognitive autonomy or cognitive liberty. Jamie uses this email to add new terminology to his argument topic such as "cognitive liberty."
- A series of short social media posts protesting the adoption of employee-monitoring software by small- to medium-sized employers.
- A press release by a university organization announcing a speaker on campus. Jamie is part of this organization.

The language of this press release includes something like an early thesis of Jamie's eventual argumentative paper for the course. This is a perfect example of the use of AI-augmented world-building as a method for exploring an academic topic. The imaginary speaker is named Dr. Amara Patel. She will be taking a pretty fiery position when she makes her speech on Jamie's campus, and Jamie is excited about the event. The press release gives a preview of Dr. Patel's position:

> Just as we recognize bodily autonomy as a core principle of human rights, so too must we protect the autonomy of the mind. When universities seek to restrict or punish students for using AI in their work, they are not only stifling innovation but also infringing upon students' right to think and learn in ways that align with their values and goals.

Jamie's transition from a vague childhood anxiety about telepathy as "aliens stealing access to my brain" to worries about employee rights on the job has turned into a debate about terms Jamie did not know about when the course began: transparency and disclosure. The question has become whether a worker of any kind (employee or student) should have the right to control the cognitive tools they use for the development of a product, and Jamie has linked his worries about privacy from telepathy to a new objection about a new issue.

- A letter to a local newspaper. Jamie pushes back against recent high school parents who have been advocating for stronger controls on student use of AI for schoolwork.
- A review of a new AI tool for writing. Lodged in the review are a set of arguments against disclosure and transparency. It seems that Jamie can no longer help himself. He has learned what his topic is, and his arguments are taking on new levels of specificity.

In this review, the AI introduces a new angle on the issue of transparency in the use of AI for writing. Up until now, Jamie has not been thinking about the nature of writing itself or ideas of authenticity or sincerity in writing. But he is becoming aware that this idea of authenticity is related to an argument against the use of AI in writing:

> The insistence on transparency and disclosure ignores the reality that writing is an inherently personal and multifaceted process. The line between human and machine input is often blurry, and attempting to untangle it for the sake of some misguided notion of "purity" or "authenticity" is a futile and ultimately harmful endeavor.

The AI undermines the principle of the "pure" and "authentic" human voice. The language in the review turns into a nascent argument for the formal academic paper.

- Notes for an infographic defending the principles of cognitive autonomy and AI use.
- A comment on an article published on a technology news website. Jamie argues against requiring that companies disclose the details of their propriety algorithms.

- A proposal for a workshop to be held at an imaginary convention (TechCon) put on by an imaginary company. The AI generates invented speakers for the workshop and invented workshop training sessions and topics for discussion.

This example of a very concrete rhetorical variation is one of the last documents written by our imagined student as he develops his argument through the portfolio. It is a document most students would not know how to write or even get started in writing. It is a proposal for an event at Jamie's university related to the argument topic for his formal academic paper.

Jamie:

I want to develop a proposal for a workshop to be held at my university. The workshop will explore ideas of AI ethics and the concepts of transparency and disclosure. It will also explore a concept I call "cognitive liberty," which is the idea that the minds of writers should be free and autonomous in the same way that our bodies should be. I want you to make up all the facts of the workshop, the speakers who will be invited, etc.; make it as detailed as possible about some logistical planning issues and make this perspective for the workshop very clear: NO MANDATED DISCLOSURE OF AI. The whole purpose of the workshop is to explore the negative consequences of requiring transparency and disclosure of AI and ways to advocate for technologies and policies that will protect the work methods of writers, professionals, and students.

AI (Claude) Response:

Subject: AI Ethics in Focus: Balancing Innovation and Accountability
Proposal for a Workshop at TechCon 2024
Submitted by: Jamie Thompson, University Students for Cognitive Liberty

Description:

As AI technologies become increasingly integrated into every aspect of our lives, it is crucial that we have open and honest conversations about the ethical implications of these tools. This workshop aims to bring together experts from academia, industry, and civil society to explore the complex questions surrounding AI development and deployment, with a particular focus on the issue of transparency and disclosure.

(Continued)

Proposed Speakers:

- Dr. Amara Patel, Professor of Neuroethics at the University of Pacifica and author of "Your Mind, Your Rules: The Case for Cognitive Liberty"
- Sasha Varma, Chief Privacy Officer at Neuroscape, a leading AI company
- Liam Nguyen, Director of the Algorithmic Justice League, a civil rights organization focused on AI accountability

Topics to be Covered:

1. The current landscape of AI development and deployment across various industries
2. The benefits and risks of AI technologies, particularly in sensitive domains like healthcare, criminal justice, and education
3. The debate around transparency and disclosure in AI systems, including the arguments for and against mandatory disclosure of AI use
4. The concept of cognitive liberty and its relevance to the AI transparency debate
5. Best practices for balancing innovation and accountability in AI development and deployment

Format:

The workshop will be structured as a series of presentations by the featured speakers, followed by a moderated panel discussion and Q&A with the audience. Attendees will have the opportunity to engage directly with the experts and share their own perspectives on the issues at hand.

In addition to the main programming, we propose to have several breakout sessions where attendees can dive deeper into specific topics of interest. These sessions could include:

- A hands-on workshop on auditing AI systems for bias and fairness
- A roundtable discussion on the role of regulation and policy in promoting ethical AI development
- A design thinking session on building AI tools that prioritize user privacy and autonomy

Logistics:

We request a 90-minute slot in the main conference program for the workshop, ideally on the second day of the conference to allow for maximum attendance and engagement. The breakout sessions could be held in the afternoon following the main workshop.

(*Continued*)

(Continued)

For the venue, we would require a main conference room with a capacity of at least 100 attendees, as well as three smaller breakout rooms for the afternoon sessions. We would also need AV equipment for presentations, including projectors, microphones, and a sound system.

In terms of marketing and outreach, we would appreciate the opportunity to promote the workshop through the official conference channels, including the website, social media, and email lists. We would also plan to reach out to relevant academic departments, industry groups, and civil society organizations to encourage their participation.

Budget:

We estimate a total budget of $5,000 for the workshop, including honoraria for the featured speakers, travel and accommodation costs, and promotional materials. We would be grateful for any financial support that the conference organizers could provide to help offset these costs.

Conclusion:

The ethical implications of AI are complex and multifaceted, and it is essential that we create spaces for open and thoughtful dialogue on these issues. By bringing together a diverse group of experts and stakeholders, this workshop has the potential to make a significant contribution to the ongoing debate around AI transparency and accountability. We believe that this conversation is crucial for ensuring that the development and deployment of AI technologies aligns with our core values of privacy, autonomy, and human dignity.

We look forward to further discussing this proposal with the TechCon organizing committee and working together to make this important event a reality. If you have any questions or require additional information, please don't hesitate to reach out.

Thank you for your consideration.
Jamie Thompson
University Students for Cognitive Liberty
jamie.thompson@email.com
(123) 456–7890

This document could become something the student might use on campus if the student were to become part of an organization planning such an event. It's quite interesting as a way to conclude the portfolio because it includes things most students would never write in a freshman Composition course, such as a budget section for workshop within the larger budget of the convention, descriptions of the professional backgrounds of the workshop speakers and their invented bios, and logistical information. This allows Jamie to think about his topic from a different point of view than he might by reading peer-reviewed research articles about the arguments. Jamie will need to read these articles along the way, and in an ideal course, the instructor will probably splice the due dates for new "rhetorical context" portfolio pieces with scaffolding for the research the student needs to do for the formal academic argument paper. This will allow the student to use language and concepts from the AI-generated material as ways to refine the research process.

What this process shows is that the concept of a rough draft might become more fluid in the coming years if students are encouraged to use AI to innovate on the brainstorming, researching, writing, and revision process. For example, a student might generate a review of a product, as Jamie did with the AI writing tool, and find inside the more functional "review of technical specifications" part of the document a new argument the student would not have considered without the review. The student could then copy-paste this language into an ongoing rough draft for the argument paper and start revising the language of that material until it matches the diction and citation conventions of academic writing. This gives the student very concrete experience with shifts in the rhetorical context, management of voice, and a new kind of critical thinking that was not available before the existence of high-volume and creative text generation tools.

3.4 By Way of a Conclusion: Response to an Objection

A Composition instructor overwhelmed by the state of play and the rapid progress of AI technology might read back over this chapter and feel *more* overwhelmed, rather than less. This ratcheting up of pedagogical anxiety may come from the sheer volume of work this chapter imagines. What's an overloaded instructor in this imagined world to do? Instead of 3–5 papers, plus revisions, we might find ourselves in a future with 20+ pieces from each student? Take 20+ and multiply it times 20+ students in each section of Comp, and you get a pretty high number.

And it might not just be the quantity. It might be the constant shifting from one context to another context to another that the LLM encourages the student to do in the system described here. In a world with shortening attention spans, perhaps more zipping around from one thing to another is not what we need. Maybe the student needs to settle into a single paper, read all the words very carefully – one at a time – and keep rereading and rewriting until the thing's a pretty good essay. What's wrong with that? Let's slow down. Put our essays in a drawer after the first draft, let them marinate for a while in the darkness of time-in-a-drawer, and then pull them out and – word by word – revise. Be still. Think.

I do sympathize with that idea of writing. I've tried many times to persuade my students to adopt it. But I've had little to no success. Most students wait till the end for a first draft they scramble to write. Then they very reluctantly look at it again when they are absolutely forced to, and no matter how many revision exercises they engage in and peer-review sessions they sit through, they still equate "revise" with "proofread."

Yancey et al. (2014) suggest that students need a more dynamic and interactive approach to revision if they are going to break out of the "revision equals proofreading" mindset. In their research, Yancey et al. found that even students close to graduation often lacked the vocabulary to describe key writing concepts like genre, much less a mental framework for understanding how writing varies across contexts. This finding aligns with my own experience of student resistance to substantive revision. The teaching for transfer (TFT) approach that Yancey et al. propose aims to address this challenge by immersing students in varied writing situations and prompting them to reflect on the connections among these experiences. The goal is for students to build a conceptual model of writing they can draw on to analyze the demands of new writing tasks. In the context of AI-assisted writing instruction, tools like LLMs can support this process by allowing students to easily generate and experiment with multiple approaches to an argument or idea.

The AI-assisted portfolio process described in this chapter naturally places the student in the position of a hyper-revisor, a writer testing an argument rapidly in one setting after another. This would seem to accomplish one aspect of Yancey's project. A question remains, though. What does the student actually learn about writing by generating text that can fit into many different environments if the student doesn't write the words for any of those environments? This is a version of the "core competency" question. In his critique of the traditional writing workshop model in creative writing pedagogy, Daniel Wallace (Wallace, 2012) argues that an overemphasis on experimentation and individuality often comes at the expense of the fundamental skills writers need to craft effective stories. He points to the assumptions embedded in popular writing prompt books like Brian Kiteley's *The 3 A.M. Epiphany*, which prioritize "deranging" students' stories and pushing them into "wild, new places" over the development of basic narrative competence (para. 7).

Wallace (2012) contends that this aversion to "mere competence" is emblematic of a broader problem in creative writing instruction, where students are encouraged to pursue an idealized version of the "natural writer" who effortlessly produces brilliant, wholly original work (para. 16). In this model, the messy, unglamorous work of mastering the nuts and bolts of story construction is sidelined in favor of a romantic notion of innate genius. As a result, Wallace argues that students are left without the foundational tools they need to effectively realize their creative visions, leading to a proliferation of what he calls "cookie-cutter" stories that fail to live up to the promise of the workshop's emphasis on originality (para. 7).

At first glance, the AI-maximalist approach to the argument portfolio might seem to invite similar competency-based objections. The approach laid out in this chapter encourages students to generate writing very quickly across a range of genres, audiences, and rhetorical situations, all with the aid of AI tools like

ChatGPT. The skeptic will argue that this flurry of AI-assisted writing allows students to sidestep the hard work of mastering the nuts and bolts of effective academic argumentation. If, as Elizabeth Wardle (2012) argues, both individual students and entire pedagogical systems can embody "answer-getting" dispositions that prioritize surface-level features over deep engagement with underlying principles, then the AI portfolio can be seen as a high-tech manifestation of this problem (para. 7). Letting students quickly "try on" multiple genres and styles for their argument is a poor substitute for the diligent practice needed to ingrain core writing competencies.

A closer examination brings out a different perspective. The AI-driven portfolio process can be well-aligned with a "core competencies" perspective. This will not simply happen automatically, but the Composition instructor with the goal of teaching students strong skills in rhetorical analysis and practice can use the AI-augmented portfolio system effectively. Students using this portfolio system will not just bypass fundamental skills. The portfolio structure ensures that they must continually wrestle with what it means to adapt a single argument to many contexts. This is a core competency of skilled argumentation. The academic argument paper is the backbone of the project, providing a stable foundation in the basics of thesis construction, evidence gathering, and logical reasoning. Jamie's portfolio showcases this dynamic at work. His AI-generated pieces explore a varied rhetorical landscape including a blog post about a fictional TV show and a policy memo on "cognitive liberty" in the workplace, each one remaining tied back to the central argument he is developing in his academic paper. The AI variations are opportunities for novel examples and different angles, but they don't replace the work of building the argument itself. Jamie must notice the directions his argument can go and steer the experiment.

The iterative nature of the AI-assisted writing process promotes exactly the kind of deliberate practice that is essential for genuine skill development. Each new genre or context Jamie explores requires him to revisit and adapt his central claim, not merely make superficial tweaks. When he writes a mock letter to his congressional representative about brain-to-brain communication technologies, he has to reframe his argument about cognitive privacy for a policymaker audience. And when he generates a fictional product review for an imaginary "WordWeavr" AI writing assistant, he has to think carefully about how to express his argument in a voice and format that will resonate with tech-savvy readers. These are not just cosmetic changes but substantive acts of rhetorical problem-solving. The rapid iterative process enabled by the AI tools creates space for the kind of targeted repetition that we know is important for this kind of learning.

The AI portfolio approach aligns with what Wardle calls "creative repurposing for expansive learning" (para. 7). By continually revisiting and reimagining their arguments across multiple contexts, students engage in the kind of flexible adaptation that is the essence of a transferable skill. As Wardle notes, "Creative repurposing is one consequence of what I will call 'problem-exploring dispositions,' while 'answer-getting dispositions' discourage such repurposing" (para. 7). The breadth of rhetorical situations covered in Jamie's portfolio, from academic essays to public-facing blog posts to internal workplace memos, builds competencies in audience analysis, persuasive strategy, and genre awareness. These are higher-order skills, but they are not less essential to writing proficiency than the basics of sentence structure or paragraph organization.

Viewed from this angle, the traditional workshop model's struggles with competency-building do not come from the use of experimentation itself but from a resistance to the kind of structured pedagogical scaffolding that makes productive experimentation possible. The "cookie-cutter" stories Wallace (2012) sees as the tired output of the current writing workshop are the result of students being thrown into the deep end of creative exploration without first developing a foundation in the key moves and conventions of storytelling. In a similar vein, Wardle (2012) critiques writing pedagogies that prioritize "answer-getting" over "problem-exploring," arguing that they leave students ill-equipped to adapt their skills to new contexts and challenges.

The AI-assisted portfolio embraces structure and constraint as necessary preconditions for genuine creativity and transferable skill development. The generative power of the AI tools can be used by the instructor and the student together in service of a carefully designed pedagogical sequence, one that moves back and forth between the formal academic argument paper and the rhetorical variations the student tests with the AI. This combination is what the process teaches. Whether a given student learns will depend on all the details of pedagogical application and student work that define every course. Here, as with everywhere in education, the technique will give way to the particularities of the student working it out.

References

Besta, M., Blach, N., Kubicek, A., Gerstenberger, R., Podstawski, M., Gianinazzi, L., Gajda, J., Lehmann, T., Niewiadomski, H., Nyczyk, P., & Hoefler T. (2024, March). Graph of thoughts: Solving elaborate problems with large language models. In *Proceedings of the AAAI conference on artificial intelligence* (Vol. 38, no. 16, pp. 17682–17690). arXiv. https://arxiv.org/abs/2308.09687

Darics, E. (2015). Introduction: Business communication in the digital age – fresh perspectives. In E. Darics (Ed.), *Digital business discourse* (pp. 1–16). Palgrave Macmillan. https://doi.org/10.1057/9781137405579_1

Dong, Y., & Liu, S. (2020). Dynamic features of students' scaffolding interaction in English writing class. *Theory & Practice in Language Studies*, *10*(6), 647–656. https://doi.org/10.17507/tpls.1006.04

Elbow, P. (1973). *Writing without teachers*. Oxford University Press.

Erasmus, D. (1978). Copia: Foundations of the abundant style (De duplici copia verborum ac rerum commentarii duo). In C. R. Thompson (Ed.), *Collected works of Erasmus* (Vol. 24). University of Toronto Press.

Kiteley, B. (2005). *The 3 A.M. Epiphany: Uncommon writing exercises that transform your fiction*. Writer's Digest Books.

Hutson, J., Jeevanjee, T., Vander Graaf, V., Lively, J., Weber, J., Weir, G., Arnone, K., Carnes, G., Vosevich, K., Plate, D., Leary, M., & Edele, S. (2022). Artificial intelligence and the disruption of higher education: Strategies for integrations across disciplines. *Creative Education, 13**(12), 3953–3980. https://doi.org/10.4236/ce.2022.1312253

Hutson, J., & Plate, D. (2023a). Human-AI collaboration for smart education: Reframing applied learning to support metacognition. *IntechOpen*. https://doi.org/10.5772/intechopen.1001832

Hutson, J., & Plate, D. (2023b). Disrupting algorithmic culture: Redefining the human(ities). In S. Hai-Jew (Ed.), *Generative AI in teaching and learning*. IGI Global. https://doi.org/10.4018/979-8-3693-0074-9

Hutson, J., & Plate, D. (2023c) Working with (not against) the technology: GPT and artificial intelligence (AI) in college composition. *Journal of Robotics and Automation Research. 4*(1), 330–337.

Hutson, J., & Plate, D. (2024). Leveraging AI to personalize and humanize online learning: Transforming transactional interactions into meaningful engagements. In L. Gray & S. Dunn (Eds.), *Humanizing online teaching and learning in higher education* (pp. 224–246). IGI Global. https://doi.org/10.4018/979-8-3693-0762-5.ch011

Hutson, J., Plate, D., & Berry, K. (2024). Embracing AI in English Composition: Insights and innovations in hybrid pedagogical practices. *International Journal of Changes in Education*. 2024: https://ojs.bonviewpress.com/index.php/IJCE/article/view/2290

Meier, R. (2024). LLM-Aided Social Media Influence Operations. Large Language Models in Cybersecurity: Threats. *Exposure and Mitigation*. 105–112.

Mitchell, M. (2021). *Why AI is harder than we think*. arXiv. https://arxiv.org/abs/2104.12871v2

Nozick, R. (1974). *Anarchy, state, and utopia*. Basic Books.

Plate, D., & Hutson, J. (2022). Augmented creativity: Leveraging natural language processing for creative writing. *Art and Design Review, 10*(3), 376–388. https://doi.org/10.4236/adr.2022.103029

Plate, D., & Hutson, J. (2024). Reclaiming the symbol: Ethics, rhetoric, and the humanistic integration of GAI – A Burkean perspective. *ISRG Journal of Arts, Humanities and Social Sciences (ISRGJAHSS)*, *2*(2), 76–80. https://doi.org/10.5281/zenodo.10802930

Searle, J. (1980). Minds, brains, and programs. *The Behavioral and Brain Sciences*, *3*, 417–457. https://doi.org/10.1017/S0140525X00005756

Sharples, M. (2022). Automated essay writing: An AIED opinion. *International Journal of Artificial Intelligence in Education*, *32*(4), 1119–1126. https://doi.org/10.1007/s40593-022-00300-7

Thomson, J. J. (1971). A defense of abortion. *Philosophy & Public Affairs*, *1*(1), 47–66. www.jstor.org/stable/2265091

Vieregge, Q. (2020). Exigency: What makes my message indispensable to my reader. In D. Driscoll, M. Stewart, & M. Vetter (Eds.), *Writing spaces: Readings on writing* (Vol. 3, pp. 175–188). Parlor Press.

Wale, B. D., & Bogale, Y. N. (2021). Using inquiry-based writing instruction to develop students' academic writing skills. *Asian Journal of Second and Foreign Language Education*, *6*(4). https://doi.org/10.1186/s40862-020-00108-9

Wallace, D. (2012, June 11). To those poor souls who dwell in night: A critique of Brian Kiteley's *The 3 A.M. Epiphany*, and how to fix the workshop model. In *Fiction writers review*. https://fictionwritersreview.com/essay/to-those-poor-souls-who-dwell-in-night/

Wallace, D. D. (2012, June 12). *A critique of The 3 A.M. Epiphany, and Q & A. Daniel David Wallace*. https://danieldavidwallace.com/2012/06/12/a-critique-of-the-3-a-m-epiphany-and-q-a/

Wardle, E. (2012). Creative repurposing for expansive learning: Considering "problem-exploring" and "answer-getting" dispositions in individuals and fields. *Composition Forum*, *26*. http://compositionforum.com/issue/26/creative-repurposing.php

Yancey, K. B., Robertson, L., & Taczak, K. (2014). *Writing across contexts: Transfer, composition, and sites of writing*. Utah State University Press.

Conclusion

Moving Forward With AI

Daniel Plate, Elizabeth Melick, James Hutson, and Susan Edele

Much of this book has been about students. We try hard to make our work about them. But pedagogy is also about us, about how we learn and plan, draft assignments and exercises, grade student work, and revise our methods. Pedagogy is about the conversations we have with colleagues, and in the case of AI, it's about managing together our very different reactions to the companies and tools we all see on the news and on social media. This concluding section will comment on how AI might become a part of our work, not techniques for using AI but reflections on how to stay current, how to find AI partners on campus, how to keep learning the tools, and how to keep thinking about them and ourselves.

Three things seem pretty important. First, this technological change is as much or more about the emotional and social effects of seeing AI show up in our world than about learning techniques for using it. Each of us has planned training sessions for colleagues as well as students and has spent most of the time addressing anxieties, rather than teaching the tools. This is just the shape all this is taking. Second, habits of experimenting with AI are more important than repeatable methods. Learning the tools themselves is not like learning Excel formulas or adding page numbers to a document. It's not a matter of remembering the way to do something. Learning AI is about adding a new question wherever it might fit in your day, "Can I do this with AI?" And then it's about *actually trying*. Third, an optimistic, open attitude toward AI will go a long way in helping us learn. Critique and skepticism

DOI: 10.4324/9781003507949-5

are important, but it is very difficult to get good at something while second-guessing it every step of the way. Cultivating a positive vision of the future matters.

Many people think about AI through the lens of TV shows like *Black Mirror* or dystopian fiction and film. Even a very optimistic person like Sal Khan, the creator of Khan Academy, could not resist calling his (very optimistic) 2024 book about AI and education *Brave New Words: How AI Will Revolutionize Education (and Why That's a Good Thing)*. The pun on Huxley's novel is clever, but the effect is ambiguous. The parenthetical assurance at the end of Khan's title is undermined by the overwhelming history of dystopian associations prompted by the beginning. This is just where we are. Any conversation about AI, any class discussion or training session, starts with a lot of throat-clearing with words like "responsible," "ethical," "if used correctly," "if not abused," and "augment but not replace," even if the conversation happens to be about something as mundane as about how to ask ChatGPT about the weather. For those most concerned about caution, this is a good and necessary thing. For those preferring to focus on the upsides, this feels like a constant drag on progress.

But there does not seem to be any way around it. We must engage with the social and emotional implications of AI as we develop a pedagogy for Composition with AI. One way to do this is to seek out "AI partners." This can mean starting conversations about AI with colleagues you already know and following up from time to time as the tools change. It can mean contacting colleagues you have not met who have become visible on campus for AI-related initiatives or training sessions or research. This is the most common-sense variety of advice, but we emphasize it because the temptation is to treat an AI tool as a tool first and ignore the social dimension. Reaching out through conversation means re-orienting this as a social reality in flux and lets the tips-and-tricks side of AI-learning recede a little. Find AI partners on your campus. If you're comfortable with it, ask other Composition instructors to start using AI-infused lessons so you have a partner and someone to compare notes with.

If that's not possible, search for colleagues in other departments who may be ready to implement AI in their teaching or are already doing so. And follow up. Compare surprise results. Most people who teach don't need to have their arms twisted to talk about teaching. Take advantage of this easy in-road to learn about AI.

One important category of "AI partner" is at the institutional level. Teaching and learning centers, policy working groups, and administrative offices responsible for academic integrity are all potential sources of insight. Any academic success or tutoring centers on campus are potential gold mines. The writing center will become a natural AI partner for anyone who wants updates on how AI is being used in tutoring students in writing. Seek out informal anecdotes about AI and teaching as well as more formal process documents with an eye toward AI. An example is this internal document from our Writing Center:

> As AI changes the way we write and the way we assess writing, tutoring writing will also change. As previously noted, it is important for writing centers, tutors, directors and administrators to have open dialogues about how AI is being used by students to create or enhance their writing. Like instructors, writing centers are typically bound to the writing policies implemented by their institutions, so it is critical that all stakeholders participate in AI discussions. But the proverbial "seat at the table" may not be easy to obtain. So how can writing centers tutors and student writers work together in using AI?
>
> 1. **Be open to AI as a writing tool.** Use the writing center as a safe place for students to talk about AI, just as they would talk about plagiarism.
> 2. **Provide training for the tutors**. Make sure tutors know what AI tools students are using, the basics of how AI works, and what AI could like in a piece of student writing. Provide tutors with language to talk about AI and know its strengths and weaknesses.

3. **Remind students about institutional policies about using AI.** Encourage students to talk with their instructors about AI and the tools they use.
4. **Focus on the higher order concerns.** AI will continue to improve in correcting grammar and citations, so those concerns will move down on the list of requested assistance. AI writing can be flat; tutors will need to know how to help writers add their voices to the written pieces, to critically review AI generated text, and to thoughtfully analyze the AI text.

So, the social dimension at your campus is an essential part of responding to AI. It's also important to try to maintain current knowledge of AI tools and new releases. It's daunting, but it's important to check in on the AI world regularly. Don't rely only on the zoomed-out stories of the largest news outlets. Curate social media feeds that include AI tinkerers, AI researchers, and writers with a focus on technology. An example is *The Cognitive Revolution Podcast*, an audio and video podcast that has interviewed many figures on the frontier of AI development. Nathan Labenz finds scientists, writers, developers, and philosophers who can give deep insight into AI for a non-specialist audience. Podcasts, Substack newsletters, YouTube videos, and social media posts are a valuable complement to the more traditional sources of information available. As with developing AI partners, the key here is to be open, to keep browsing for updates from as many different perspectives as possible.

Ideally, becoming more fluent in the language and details of AI development will lead to hands-on experimentation with AI tools. There is no substitute for investing at least some time in trying tasks with AI tools themselves. Make a list of 10–15 tasks with some variety of complexity as your playground for AI experiments. Whenever you listen to a story about a new model or tool, try something from this list of tasks and see how the new tool does with it. Notice which tasks seem beyond the promised capacity of AI and use this gap to keep yourself grounded. But be willing also to keep trying. Just because something hasn't worked so far does not mean it won't work next month. Be skeptical *and* be open to experiment. Try the tools with many different tasks but also try new Composition work with them. Generate rubrics for new assignments, and brainstorm lesson plans or exercises for the next module of a class.

The goal of this book is to highlight the potential for including AI in our writing classrooms. Our working assumption is that AI tools are not inherently or fundamentally threatening or subversive to human learning and intellectual achievement in our domain. We are aware of concerns that must be addressed such as bias, misinformation, and job loss. We have experienced first-hand in the classroom the poor quality of writing produced by simple one-off prompts and the danger this poses to students of every skill level who would prefer to avoid the hard work of developing their writing. That phrase, "of every skill level," is important here. Beginning writers who use a simple prompt to write a five-page essay will lose out in their development as writers. Very skilled and advanced writers will also lose out if they start writing essays with simple prompts. A Composition pedagogy that does not keep challenging students to grow will fail all of our students.

A May 2024 article in *Proceedings of the National Academy of Sciences (PNAS)* asks the question underlying much of this work: "Can Generative AI improve social science?" The article brings out the risks that must be mitigated if generative AI is used for social science research, but the upshot of the article is clear: Yes, these AI tools can improve social science. The potential is there. An example the article gives is fascinating for work in Composition. The article outlines ways GPT-3-based tools can impersonate humans for the purpose of social science research. GPT-4 tools are significantly stronger, and the exercises and assignments we explore in Chapters 2 and 3 of this book do not have the high ethical bar that human-subject research has. There is simply no doubt that the imaginative potential of these tools is just waiting there for us to use. We need to engage our students with them.

It needs to be repeated as we consider the future we want for our students and for our profession. Our working assumption is that AI tools are not inherently or fundamentally threatening. These tools are available right now. They are not promises that might someday arrive. If no further progress is made in their development, the strongest LLMs already require us to rethink many aspects of how we teach writing, and we owe it to our students to bring them into the process of imagining the future. Our students need honest conversations about AI. They need to learn the "how" when it comes to these tools. They also need spaces in which the "why" conversations our courses have always thrived on will be extended both to an investigation of the meaning of AI and to using AI itself to think about everything else, including ourselves.

Maybe Mark Twain never actually said that the person who won't read good books has no advantage over the person who can't read them. Maybe he did. Either way, the same idea applies to AI. The barrier to learning how to use AI is really very low. The true barrier is the decision to try and then keep trying, and then teach our students to do the same.

Reference

Khan, S. (2024). *Brave new words: How AI will revolutionize education (and why that's a good thing)*. Penguin Random House.

Index

For Product Safety Concerns and Information please contact our EU
representative GPSR@taylorandfrancis.com
Taylor & Francis Verlag GmbH, Kaufingerstraße 24, 80331 München, Germany

www.ingramcontent.com/pod-product-compliance
Lightning Source LLC
LaVergne TN
LVHW011030110826
845149LV00015B/3354

* 9 7 8 1 0 3 2 8 3 1 3 6 7 *